Christian Education
and the Search for Meaning

Christian Education and the Search for Meaning

Jim Wilhoit

Second Edition

BAKER BOOK HOUSE
Grand Rapids, Michigan

Copyright 1986, 1991 by
Baker Book House Company.
Published 1986. Second Edition 1991

Printed in the United States of America

Library of Congress Cataloging-in-Publication Data

Wilhoit, Jim.
   Christian education and the search for meaning / Jim Wilhoit. — 2nd ed.
     p. cm.
   Includes bibliographical references and index.
   ISBN 0-8010-9711-8
   1. Christian education. I. Title
   BV1464.W49 1991
   268'.01–dc20   91-26232
                                           CIP

Unless otherwise noted, all Scripture references are taken from the
Holy Bible, New International Version. Copyright © 1973, 1978, 1984
International Bible Society. Used by permission of Zondervan Bible
Publishers. Other versions cited include the King James Version (KJV), the
New American Standard Bible (NASB), the New Testament in Modern
English (Phillips), and the Revised Standard Version (RSV).

Contents

=1=

Purpose in Christian Education

Christian education is in crisis. It is not healthy and vital; as a discipline, it is bankrupt. To say that a discipline is bankrupt is not to claim that it is worthless or that its scholars are not diligently working, but rather that the discipline is not doing what it is supposed to do (see Wink 1973, p. 1). Christian education maintains a façade of viability. It employs a host of trained workers and supports an impressive variety of workshops, conferences, and other activities. Yet all too often it exhibits the fatal flaw of having no clear purpose.

The Current Lack of Purpose

The current crisis in Christian education stems, in large measure, from a lack of clear purpose at the grassroots level. The people most directly involved in Christian education—Sunday-school teachers, youth counselors, and Bible-study leaders—often have no idea of the ultimate purpose of their educational endeavors. The teacher of an adult class may be told that the curriculum for the next quarter is a study of the Book of Acts. Yet the reason for selecting Acts—or for studying Isaiah during the current quarter—may be clear to no one. Or consider a children's department where most of the time is spent on crafts and workbooks that have only an incidental relationship to the Bible passage of the week. The teachers believe that they should not bore the children, so they do their best to make the class a lot of fun. Often, however, no one knows the ultimate purpose for the class. Such a lack of purpose can devastate the personnel in ministries where the results are slow in coming and where faithful work often goes unnoticed.

Directors of Christian education are typically pressed for time and consequently tend to focus their energies on immediate problems, ignoring the need for long-range goals. For the average director, cultivating a sense of purpose among the lay workers is an item of low priority. Education directors may say that a vision for the teachers will become clear if the Christian-education program sticks with the Bible, or they may claim that teachers need methods, not clear purposes. But these program directors do not seem to realize that the question of how to teach can be adequately answered only after settling the question of the goal of teaching. Method is no substitute for purpose; indeed, if method becomes the primary focus, Christian education is reduced to a mere technique. A sense of purpose is no needless luxury. Yet the current focus on the urgent and the immediately relevant has too often deprived Christian educators of a needed sense of direction.

There are several ways in which having a common purpose and vision greatly enhances the effectiveness of educational ministries:

A sense of purpose acts as a sentinel guarding the resources of the educational team from being siphoned off into areas of ministry that are worthwhile, but secondary.

Team members come to see that what they are doing, however simple and mundane it may appear, is vitally important work—changing lives, healing souls, helping people discover meaning in life.

The team is alerted to and thus can avoid inappropriate ministry practices.

Encouraged to ask the question, "What method and strategy best fit our common purpose?" the team is freed from a mentality that would merely maintain the status quo to develop ministries that are on the cutting edge.

A common purpose helps maintain a truly Christ-centered and educationally effective ministry.

Regrettably, some evangelicals have considered themselves exempt from being concerned about purpose. "After all," they say, "we teach the Bible." "Teaching the Bible," however, means many different things to different people. It may entail a variety of sub-Christian and humanistic educational orientations which well-meaning Christians adopted during their school days and later imposed unconsciously on their "Bible teaching." Other educators are content simply to pour Bible facts into their students' heads. It is thus inadequate to define the purpose of Christian education as merely to "teach the Bible."

The effects of purposelessness plague Christian-education programs. Many programs, for example, face a lack of volunteers. Often, moreover, a veneer of activity only partially hides a lack of direction that has demoralized both lay and professional staff. Why should people volunteer for a job that seems purposeless? Christian educators have failed to see that programs and activities in themselves are worthless. There must be a purpose for the efforts that lay workers put forth. Good communication skills, engaging methods, and well-conceived curricula should serve the basic purpose, not replace it.

The Business of Christian Education

Christian education is dedicated to helping people discover God's meaning for life. It aims to enable them to gain a liberating perspective and lifestyle. Two points call for special attention here: (1) Christian education is a people-intensive ministry; and (2) it focuses on the meaning of life.

In the work of Christian education, the greatest resource is the people who teach and disciple others. To maintain effective ministry, we must learn, as the best corporations have already learned, that the key to any business is its people, and our leadership must focus on shaping their values. "Every excellent company . . . is clear on what it stands for, and takes the process of value shaping seriously" (Peters and Waterman 1982, p. 280). In the most successful companies certain values permeate the corporate structure, giving direction to employees and programs. The executives know that the future of their corporation is largely dependent upon the values that their employees hold toward the customer and their work. One of the important tasks of a director of Christian education is to shape the values of the people who make up the Christian-education team. The values that teachers carry into the classroom matter far more than the curriculum they follow. A director cannot "teacher-proof" an educational program, because a teacher's values will be caught by the student, even if they are not overtly taught. The teacher's values control the "hidden curriculum"—the shape, feel, and hidden agenda of the class, which may confirm or deny the material being explicitly taught. The primary leadership function of the director of Christian education, then, is to shape the values of those who teach.

At Disney World great efforts are made to have every employee understand the purpose of the business—to make people happy. From the first day on the job, that theme is driven home, and the employees come to share the vision. The same should be true in Christian education, which aims at helping people gain a comprehensive view of God's world and the meaning and purpose of life. If program directors can communicate their commitment to helping people find meaning in life, then teachers and other workers will catch the vision.

Program directors can take several steps to ensure that an appropriate emphasis will be placed on people:

Make use of what is available. Teachers want to improve education by somehow getting better students, and students want to improve their schooling by getting better teachers. But we must start with the resources we have been given. Consequently, we should focus on teacher development rather than teacher replacement.

Give teacher training and affirmation top priority.

Nurture the character and spiritual lives of the teachers.

Take modeling seriously. Encourage teachers to be open with their students about how they seek to live their life faithfully before God in the midst of difficulties and setbacks.

Choose a curriculum for its ability to help teachers teach rather than for its eye appeal or ease of use.

In addition to being people-intensive, Christian education helps students make sense out of life. The English word *educate* can be traced back to the Latin word *educere*, "to lead out." This etymology reminds us that education is the process of leading students from where they are to a place where they can see the world—including the spiritual and the natural dimensions—in a more accurate way. To lead students to a more Christian view of life and the world, the Christian educator must understand students as they are, the goals they should be guided toward, and the best means to achieve these goals. Above all, he or she should be guiding them in the search for meaning.

Modern men and women, particularly in our secular and humanistic society, deeply yearn for a sense of purpose. Not just philosophers but all adults earnestly seek the purpose of life. Some people may never phrase the precise question "What is life about?" but their experimentation with various lifestyles, their use of drugs, their preoccupation with sex, power, and money, show that they are asking the question. The common query "What are you into?" is a question about meaning. People who were desperately searching for personal meaning have asked me this question, hoping, I believe, that my answer might both provide them with something they could "get into" and give them a sense of purpose. In past generations a set of certain common values provided many individuals with a sense of meaning and purpose. Our modern society, however, with its decadent values has no deeply satisfying purpose to offer searching men and women.

After a time of searching in vain for a sense of purpose, people generally tire of asking ultimate questions and settle for any meaning that is at hand in order to get on with life. They declare a moratorium on the search and most often accept the prevailing values of the culture. In the bustle of everyday activities, short-term goals become more important than the search for meaning.

It would be unwise to say that Christian education seeks to give a person meaning or to answer all questions. Rather, Christian education can facilitate the search for personal meaning and, in helping people detect God's purpose for life, can most certainly suggest answers. Ultimately, however, meaning is found by individuals themselves and not given to them. Viktor Frankl reminds us that "man's search for meaning is a primary force in his life. . . . The meaning of our existence is not invented by ourselves, but rather detected" (1963, pp. 154, 157).

A Christian-education program that focuses on the meaning of life will display certain distinct characteristics:

There is a constant effort to connect the Bible and life.

Concentration on just one alone is insufficient for a meaning-centered Christian education.

Personal meaning is discovered by the students, not given to them. Each individual constructs his or her meaning for life—it can't just be handed over. The teacher serves as a construction superintendent giving wise and biblical advice, but letting the students discover God's plan for their own lives.

Faithful Christian living is a higher priority than Bible knowledge or doctrinal precision.

Classes are designed to be a place of safety and grace where people sense that they are part of a caring network.

This book proposes an aim for Christian education that incorporates both biblical insights and key findings from the social sciences. In chapter 2 we will discuss biblical themes that bear on the purpose of Christian education. The next chapter examines the basic theological concepts that must be adopted if Christian education is to achieve its aim. Chapter 4 evaluates three contemporary secular approaches to education; chapter 5 introduces an alternative that attempts to measure up to the biblical standard. The next two chapters discuss the relation of the social sciences to Christian education; after a few general concerns have been identified and recommendations made for relating the two fields, we will look at specific findings from the social sciences and consider how these apply to classroom instruction. Finally, chapter 8 integrates theology, educational theory, and social science into an evangelical theory of biblical instruction.

2

Biblical Foundations: Priesthood, Servanthood, and God's Transforming Grace

Christian education is in the business of helping people find meaning in life through highly personal teaching ministries. In the "ministry for meaning" it works in conjunction with preaching, counseling, worship, mission, evangelism, and social service, all of which can contribute to a person's sense of purpose. Ideally, a theory of Christian education should grow out of three biblical themes that relate directly to a Christian's sense of meaning: the priesthood of all believers, with its privileges and responsibilities; the call to serve others; and the power of God's grace for personal renewal.

The Priesthood of All Believers

The doctrine of the priesthood of all believers can be called the Magna Carta of Christian education. This doctrine mandates and enables Christian education and serves as its implicit theological foundation. When properly understood, the biblical principle that all believers are priests has infused Christian education with a refreshing vitality and spirit of renewal; at other times, however, it has been used to excuse individualism and intellectual lethargy. A balanced concept of the priesthood of all believers will affirm the personal spiritual responsibility of all Christians, their right and duty to minister in Christ's name, and the truth that one does not abide in Christ apart from abiding in the body of Christ, the church.

Access to Christ

Martin Luther (1483–1546) saw the doctrine of the priesthood of all believers as being grounded in the finished redemptive work of Christ. In his view, Christ's death and its benefits, received through grace by faith, are completely available to every contrite believer. Salvation thus comes through personal surrender to Christ and not through sacraments administered by priests. Luther believed that Christ no longer needed to be sacrificed in the mass and that therefore the need for an exclusive priesthood had vanished. The view that the completed work of Christ set aside the sacrificing priesthood was developed by both John Calvin (1509–1564) and Ulrich Zwingli (1484–1531). They argued that Christ's finished work cannot be repeated by the priests of the church and that his salvific activity is distributed through faith to all persons who trust in him. In a sermon entitled "Of the Clarity and Certainty of the Word of God," Zwingli explained that the "royal priesthood" of 1 Peter 2 means "that the Lord Jesus has called all Christians to kingly honour and to the priesthood, so that they do not need a sacrificing priest to offer on their behalf" (1953, p. 88). The spiritual accessibility of Christ serves as the bedrock for the doctrine of the priesthood of all believers. Luther, Calvin, and Zwingli all emphasized the truth that Christ's salvific benefits do not require mediation through a priest but can be received directly by any spiritually receptive and renewed person.

This emphasis on direct access to Christ should not be misconstrued as a license for individualism. Zwingli went on in his sermon to identify the basic implication of the New Testament concept of universal priesthood, namely, the responsibility incumbent upon all believers to exercise their spiritual gifts in ministry for the benefit of the church. He wrote, "They are all priests, offering [their] spiritual gifts, that is, dedicating themselves wholly to God" (1953, p. 88). The vocation of believer-priests is to serve others and to worship God through the gifts God has given them.

The Implication of Spiritual Responsibility

Luther recognized that if all Christians are called to be responsible servants and worshipers, they must be trained and equipped to fulfil this calling. Hence he became involved in Christian education. His famous Small Catechism stands as a reminder of this interest. The Small Catechism was written after he visited nearby country parishes, where he was appalled by the ignorance he found even among the clergy. It is said that after Luther had made a reference to the Decalogue, one minister asked if that was a new book. In the preface to his catechism, Luther expresses his concern about the religious training of the laity:

> The deplorable condition in which I found religious affairs during a recent visitation of the congregations has impelled me to publish this Catechism, or statement of the Christian doctrine, after having prepared it in very brief and simple terms. Alas! What misery I beheld! The people, especially those who live in the villages, seem to have no knowledge whatever of Christian doctrine, and many of the pastors are ignorant and incompetent teachers.

Luther was keenly aware that, since all Christians are priests, each individual believer must ultimately answer to Christ concerning his or her own spiritual condition. Thus the sheer ignorance of so many of the Christians of his day shocked him. If these people were accountable for their faith, then, Luther reasoned, they must be instructed in spiritual matters.

Luther and the other Reformers supported education because, in part, they recognized that Christians are called to be far more than just sincerely religious. The pastor is not the only person in the parish who is to study the Scriptures and to seek actively to minister to others. All Christians are called to worship God, utilize their gifts, and minister to others according to God's principles as set forth in Scripture. Good intentions or ignorance of divine requirements does not absolve the believer of these responsibilities.

Philipp Jacob Spener (1635–1705) and a number of like-minded Lutheran Pietists developed further the ramifications which this doctrine has for Christian education. Spener was a brilliant and sensitive Lutheran pastor who held a doctorate in theology and was fluent in several languages, yet he also firmly believed that a vital faith is more important for ministry than is either ordination or formal training. He did not disparage theological training (although he wanted to reform it), but he deeply felt that in order to be fit for ministry, a renewed heart and mind are indispensable. He was aware that, though Lutheranism taught the doctrine of the priesthood of all believers, people still looked on the pastor as the only spiritual center and theological expert in the church. The laity, for the most part, were passive recipients of sermons and sacraments. To correct this situation, Spener, in his book *Pia Desideria*, called for an increased and "diligent exercise of the spiritual priesthood" (1964, p. 92).

Spener went on to note that the responsibilities of the spiritual priesthood cluster in three general areas. (1) It is the duty of every Christian "industriously to study in the Word of the Lord." By spending time in study of Scripture we can order our lives by its priorities and minister the word of truth to those around us. (2) As Christians all of us have a responsibility "to teach others, especially those under [our] own roof, to chastise, exhort, convert, and edify them, to observe their life, pray for all, and in so far as possible be concerned about their salvation." Spener, like the writer to the Hebrews (5:12), believed that all Christians have a responsibility to teach in the sense of speaking the word of truth and influencing people to walk in the paths of righteousness. (3) "Every Christian is bound not only to offer himself but also what he has, his prayer, thanksgiving, good works, alms." The wonderful privileges of the universal priesthood enable us to serve others with a renewed vigor and enthusiasm and with a full array of spiritual tools. Through intercessory prayer and acts of mercy believer-priests serve one another and their world.

Spener saw his emphasis on the universal priesthood as simply a restatement of Luther's work: "Nobody can read Luther's writings with some care without observing how earnestly the sainted man advocated this spiritual priesthood" (1964, p. 92). Spener thought that an emphasis on the universal priesthood of believers is necessary for the church to fulfil its biblical obligations of service, worship, care, witness, and prayer. He did not see such a priesthood as competing with the paid clergy; rather, together they can accomplish what neither one can do alone: "No damage will be done to the ministry by a proper use of this priesthood. In fact, one of the principal reasons why the ministry cannot accomplish all that it ought is that it is too weak without the help of the universal priesthood" (p. 94). Without an emphasis on laypersons teaching other laypersons, modern Christian education would not have developed. The task of Christian education can never fall entirely upon professionals, for a church could never afford to hire all the personnel necessary to staff an adequate Christian-education program. Christians must recognize, then, that their pastor is not solely responsible for their personal religious training; their own priesthood entails various responsibilities in this area.

The Implications for Christian Education: Equipping for Spiritual Service

The priesthood of all believers places equipping for spiritual service at the heart of the church's educational ministry. This focus of Christian education must be emphasized for all ages. To live as a Christian entails carrying out the responsibilities of a believer-priest, and this is as true for an elementary-school child as for an adult.

We should note here that the consumer emphasis in modern American religion is diametrically opposed to the Reformation concept of the believer-priest. The educational ministry of a church will never be fully effective if people come to the church simply to consume spiritual benefits in exchange for their money and loyalty. By contrast, equipping means training people "to do." In the church, people must be trained for responsible priestly service. This means that we cannot be content simply to exhort people to pray, but we must teach them how to pray. And we must not merely talk about evangelism, but we must train people to share their faith.

In equipping for spiritual service, the church should give much attention to the two primary contexts in which people live out their faith, namely, the home and the marketplace. It must enable people to live as Christians bearing witness to their faith and genuinely serving their co-workers. It must also help them minister in and through their families.

Spiritual Responsibility and Personal Meaning

Many persons today are frantically searching for personal meaning. In a transient and normless society that daily witnesses atrocities around the world and lives with the constant threat of nuclear destruction, many people implicitly doubt that life has significance. Even the apparently well-adjusted have moments of doubt about meaning, because life's inevitable loss and pain disturb a hedonistic society that finds meaning basically in pleasure and prosperity. The priesthood of all believers, however, is a truth that can establish meaning in life and affirms God's original testimony that humankind was created "very good" (Gen. 1:31). Yet a sense of meaninglessness has spread like a spiritual plague, and many persons live in despair.

One of the greatest steps we can take toward giving persons a sense of meaning and purpose is to affirm that what they choose matters, that it affects their lives and the lives of others. Many today, of course, deny that humankind can make significant choices. Psychologist B. F. Skinner, for example, in his book *Beyond Freedom and Dignity*, denies that humans possess personal freedom and the dignity of making meaningful choices. Skinner sees humans as products of environmental conditioning who should neither be praised nor punished for their personal situations because "scientific analysis shifts the credit as well as the blame to the environment" (1971, p. 19). For Skinner, our lives are shaped through "control exercised by the environment" and not by genuine human choice. Humans do not make choices; they merely appear to choose as they respond to the environment. Skinner is absolutely correct when he says that if his position were allowed to shape social policy, it would take humans beyond freedom and dignity, but he fails to tell his readers that a mechanistic despair lies beyond the freedom and dignity he so despises.

Viktor Frankl is much closer to the truth when he says, "Man is *not* fully conditioned and determined. . . . Man does not simply exist, but always decides what his existence will be, what he will become in the next moment" (1963, p. 206). Frankl's observations on human life seem more insightful than Skinner's and bear the mark of a deep integrity formed through his practice of psychiatry and the three years he spent in brutal concentration camps:

We who lived in concentration camps can remember the men who walked through the huts comforting others, giving away their last piece of bread. They may have been few in number, but they offer sufficient proof that everything can be taken from a man but one thing: the last of the human freedoms—to choose one's attitude in any given set of circumstances, to choose one's own way. [p. 104]

Individuals can experience dignity only to the degree they feel that their choices make a difference in their life and the world; they must sense a responsibility for the shape of their life. Frankl reminds us that although we cannot choose our circumstances, we can determine our response to circumstances. The accusation "you made me angry" is, then, in the strictest sense, untrue, because it wrongly assumes that another person can control our emotions. Knowing that we are responsible for our own reactions to life, James urged his fellow Christians, "Consider it pure joy, my brothers, whenever you face trials of many kinds, because you know that the testing of your faith develops perseverance" (James 1:2–3).

The doctrine of the priesthood of all believers affirms human dignity and purpose by affirming spiritual responsibility. Our spiritual life is affected by our decisions, and we are accountable for these choices. The responsibility for a person's spiritual life cannot be shifted to a spouse, parent, pastor or priest, or counselor. Each individual believer is important to God's work and must act responsibly before God.

Servanthood: Serving God and Others

The biblical way of life is decidedly centered on others. Christian service, though, is a pathway of great joy and not one of self-annihilation. Our service begins with giving ourselves to God. All Christian service starts by acknowledging God's claim on all our property, talent, and time. We serve God in our worship, in our giving, in our study, and in our concern for others. Springing from a heart given to God, service always involves doing. The doing may be kind words, time spent with another, sacrificial giving, teaching; but in any event, the servant, like Jesus, goes about doing kind and good deeds.

God's Call to Responsible Action

Since we are priests, God expects us to live responsibly as his servants. In Genesis 1 and 2, immediately after creating Adam and Eve, God delineated humankind's major responsibilities. The focus of God's concern was on action. Later in Scripture an emphasis on affections and intentions appears, but in the final analysis God requires properly motivated action, not just good intentions or a warm heart. For this reason, Christian education must teach not just knowledge or skills but service of God through responsible action. Nicholas Wolterstorff, in his book *Educating for Responsible Action,* makes this point very clear when he writes, "Education must aim at producing alterations in what students tend (are disposed, are inclined) to do. It must aim at tendency learning" (1980, p. 15). Christianity must touch all areas of a person's life: thinking, feeling, and doing.

This emphasis on action must not be seen as implying a behaviorist orientation. The responsible actions commanded in Scripture are not simply reflex reactions to certain stimuli. The fruit of the Spirit cannot be produced by mere behavior modification. Rather, this fruit is the result of a deep knowledge of God, a stable relationship with him, and personal health and vitality. Sickly trees do not produce abundant fruit, and only the spiritually whole person produces abundant spiritual fruit.

Christians obey the call to responsible action not simply because responsible living is more satisfying than self-indulgence or hedonism, but because loyalty to Christ requires it. He desires that Christians obey his stipulations and walk humbly before him. Christians live responsibly because they have declared that "Jesus is Lord," which speaks of complete surrender and obedience to him. The confession "Jesus is Lord" is one of the oldest creeds of the church. "With this call the NT community submitted itself to its Lord, but at the same time it also confessed him as ruler of the world" (Bietenhard 1976, p. 514). The confession speaks of the Christian's willingness to have a unique world-view and value system. The Christian desires to follow God's commands—for example, "to act justly and to love mercy and to walk humbly with your God" (Mic. 6:8)—because that is what the Lord Jesus Christ desires. True acknowledgment of Jesus as Lord leads to a lifestyle based on love and obedience, not on self-satisfaction. To acknowledge Jesus as Lord is to acknowledge oneself as a servant of Jesus and of others, and to witness to the kingdom of God.

The early Christian community developed a lifestyle of sharing, compassion, and mission which it believed was a practical manifestation of the confession "Jesus is Lord." "Selling their possessions and goods, they gave to anyone as he had need. . . . They broke bread in their homes and ate together with glad and sincere hearts, praising God and enjoying the favor of all the people. And the Lord added to their number daily those who were being saved" (Acts 2:45–47).

The lordship of Christ touches all areas of life. It affects our relationship with God; accordingly, Paul enjoins, "Offer your bodies as living sacrifices, holy and pleasing to God—which is your spiritual worship" (Rom. 12:1). Christ's lordship also affects human relationships, as can be seen in Paul's warning to the Corinthians: "When you sin against your brothers . . . , you sin against Christ" (1 Cor. 8:12). Like leaven spreading through a lump of dough, the gospel is intended to touch all areas of life. The early Christians and the church at large attempted to order their lives so that in all their endeavors they acted responsibly before Jesus their Lord. They knew that God had called them to be faithful, but not necessarily successful as measured by society's standards. A focus on faithfulness rather than success does not promote mediocre ministry; rather, it provides an unshakable motivation for believers as they face a world filled with problems that, though seemingly insurmountable, must be addressed.

The Church as a Servant Community

The kingdom of God is present to the degree that persons allow God to reign over their lives. Consequently, the church should be a place where God's sovereignty is clearly manifested through the humble submission of its members to his just and righteous kingship. A church in which God reigns—in which the kingdom of God is manifest—will demonstrate four attributes: worship, compassionate service, witness, and discipling.

First, worship will characterize such a church. The church was born at Pentecost by the power of the Holy Spirit when the disciples had gathered together to worship. Throughout the Book of Acts the church is described as a worshiping community. The believers broke bread, gathered at the temple, sang, rejoiced, and prayed. They were grateful to God for their salvation, and when they gathered together they ascribed to him worth and honor. The church was born in worship, and likewise at the consummation of this age the church will give itself over to the worship of God (Rev. 7:9–17). A casual reading of Scripture or a quick glance at the daily newspaper reveals the fact that people all too often substitute idols—money, power, security—for the one living and true God. To be faithful servants means that we worship God alone.

The second characteristic is compassionate service. Christians are called by God to be instruments of his compassion and service in the world. The model of such service is Jesus, who "did not come to be served, but to serve" (Matt. 20:28) and who "made himself nothing, taking the very nature of a servant. . . . He humbled himself and became obedient to death—even death on a cross!" (Phil. 2:7–8). This example of service is to guide the church as it not only ministers to an aching world but strives to eliminate the sources of injustice, oppression, and degradation. In service the church is to use all of the gifts and resources it possesses as it seeks to minister to the entire person.

Third, the church in which the Lord reigns bears witness to its God. The church has a message of joy and hope that must be told to a troubled world: the message of divine-human reconciliation and true freedom through Jesus Christ. Witness must be in both word and deed. The faithful church must confirm the validity of its spoken and written message through its life. It must live its doctrines and show forth a contagious love. Jesus indicated that outsiders could legitimately test the truth of our message by our actions: "A new command I give you: Love one another. As I have loved you, so you must love one another. All men will know that you are my disciples if you love one another" (John 13:34–35). Christ here asserts that true love is to be the mark of the Christian community, and he assures us that its presence will be a powerful witness. In the past the church has seen the power of God displayed and has felt the renewal only he can bring. The Lord still mandates the church to take this message of salvation to all people.

Finally, and most important for Christian education, the church has the responsibility of discipling its members and people of all nations who call upon the Lord for salvation. That is to say, the church is to develop individuals who will "live lives worthy of God" (1 Thess. 2:12), who will bear witness through their lifestyle of gentle obedience to Christ and imitation of his character. Jesus' disciples exhibited just such an obedience to and imitation of him. Recall that when the disciples of John the Baptist noticed that Jesus' followers did not fast, they went to Jesus and asked, "How is it that we and the Pharisees fast, but your disciples do not fast?" (Matt. 9:14). Here we see that Jesus' disciples had patterned their lifestyle after their Teacher. This is the heart of discipleship. A disciple's thoughts and deeds reflect those of his or her master. Like Jesus' first disciples we should pattern our behavior after our Master. Then with Paul we will be able to say, "Follow my example, as I follow the example of Christ" (1 Cor. 11:1).

The Implications for Christian Education: Cultivating a Servant's Heart

As we have observed, effective Christian education cultivates an orientation centered on others. This humble and joyful service of God and others is something which can be taught as well as caught, so it must be given a deliberate place in our curriculum. To cultivate a servant's heart a Christian-education program needs to give attention to a few basic principles:

First, we teach what we know; we reproduce what we are. Servanthood is an area that blossoms when it is modeled and when it is held in high esteem by the leadership of a church.

Second, Christ's measure of a disciple is someone who gives attention to the marginal and the unlovely. Remember his words, "Whatever you did for one of the least of these brothers of mine, you did for me" (Matt. 25:40).

Finally, a church is truly a serving community when service becomes a natural part of the members' lifestyle. Of course, we must be realistic regarding what can be expected given a layperson's schedule. We also need to suggest ways in which people in all areas of life—families with young children, older persons with limited mobility—can be involved in service.

God's Transforming Grace

In our discussion of the priesthood of all believers we looked at only one-half of the equation, namely, our access to God and its attendant responsibilities. We must note here that the Old Testament priests not only approached God, but also ministered as agents of God's grace to his people. Priests make God's grace available to others. We are called as believer-priests to minister God's transforming power to others. "Each one should use whatever gift he has received to serve others, faithfully administering God's grace in its various forms" (1 Peter 4:10). That we can become agents to minister God's sustaining grace to others should transform our view of everyday activities. Our service in the home, our empathy with co-workers, our prayers, and our challenges to others are not just ways of being kind or speaking words of truth, but they are the way of making God's transforming power available. Paul urged the believers to whom he ministered to adopt this aim in life. In fact, he encouraged them by noting that something as simple as ordinary conversations can be a way in which God's power is dispensed: "Let your conversation be always full of grace, seasoned with salt, so that you may know how to answer everyone" (Col. 4:6).

Grace as a Verb

We are very familiar with the concept that grace is God's unmerited favor. We know that grace is a form of his kindness and love toward his people. We know that it is by God's grace that we have been reconciled to him, for we read in Ephesians 2:5 that God "made us alive with Christ even when we were dead in transgressions—it is by grace you have been saved." Yet grace is more than just a noun. It is far more than a description of one of God's attributes. Grace is a verb—grace is action. Grace is God's sustaining and transforming power.

The grace of God that has reconciled us and saved us is not just God's kindness, but his marvelous power that is able to remake us into new people. In the Book of Acts grace essentially equals power. Those persons who were full of grace were also full of God's power to preach and to work mighty miracles. Notice what is said of Stephen: "Now Stephen, a man full of God's grace and power, did great wonders and miraculous signs among the people" (Acts 6:8). God's powerful sustaining grace brings about transformation and healing in our lives. In a passage where the writer to the Hebrews is exhorting his readers to walk closely with Christ, he warns them not to try to hasten their Christian development through futile means like ceremonial foods, strange teachings, and mysterious ceremonies; rather, he advises, "It is good for our hearts to be strengthened by grace" (Heb. 13:9). In the church there are many ways that we can strengthen our hearts through grace. One of the most effective is wise and biblically grounded personal ministry of one believer to another.

Salvation begins with the new birth and will end with our glorification. We must remember that it is the grace of God that is working throughout all of this process to bring about our transformation into Christlikeness. With Paul we must be able to say, "But by the grace of God I am what I am, and his grace to me was not without effect. No, I worked harder than all of them—yet not I, but the grace of God that was with me" (1 Cor. 15:10). Ultimately God's grace brings about human transformation, and we must avail ourselves of the means that God has established to make his grace available to his children.

The Implications for Christian Education: Administering God's Grace Through Teaching

A Christian-education program that effectively ministers God's grace to others has several distinct characteristics. First, the teaching emphasizes grace as power. People have to learn that it is the power of God that brings about the transformation needed in their lives. Self-discipline and human endeavor play an important role as they enable us to avail ourselves of God's transforming power. But ultimately it is God's grace, and not our efforts, that brings about the profound changes.

Second, teaching sessions that serve to make God's power available are filled with worship, prayer, and praise. We must remember that Christian learning is sacramental. In learning about God and developing a clear perspective of who he is, we are better able to open ourselves fully to his power. We must aim to make our teaching sessions a channel whereby the humble can receive, take in, and be cleansed by God's sustaining grace. While the teaching itself is vital, it is far more transformational when we have put it in a context where God is exalted and where we by praising God have opened ourselves to the possibility of change.

Finally, the disciplines of prayer, fasting, meditation, Scripture reading, and an ordered church life must be taught in our classes. The gracious walk with God that is provided by these disciplines runs counter to modern culture. Accordingly, examples and time need to be provided for people to learn and practice them. Also, an exposure to the beauty and symmetry of the Christian faith, when it is well presented, can have a powerful and healing effect on a mind cluttered and disordered by the competing priorities of our culture. For that to happen, our classes will have to foster an atmosphere that encourages people to be open with one another and, in their vulnerability, to expose areas of their lives that need to be healed by God's grace.

Priests and Servants

Our lives are heavily influenced by metaphors and mental pictures. The power of images should not surprise the Christian, because the Bible is filled with rich literary devices. Biblical symbols such as the heavenly streets of gold, Jesus as the Shepherd, and the church as Christ's body move the humble believer more deeply than a more literal description can. Given the power of images, perhaps the easiest way to renew the vision and sense of purpose of Christian educators is to help them acquire new metaphors for their task.

In this book the images of the priest and the servant are prominent. These images capture the essential features of biblical Christian education. They are faithful to both the spirit and the particulars of the educational principles articulated in Scripture. The image of the priest brings to mind access to God, intercession, worship, service, responsibility, and stewardship. The image of the servant reminds us that the redeemed in Christ stand before him as responsible people who will grow in the faith as they love and serve him and others. All Christians are to be servants, witnessing in word and deed to a saving God.

The doctrine of the priesthood of all believers provides the rationale for Christian education by both mandating and enabling it. The doctrine mandates Christian education through its implication that each Christian is responsible to God for his or her own growth. It places upon each of us the responsibility to learn more of God and to support others in their search for meaning in a confused world. Rather than depending on a professional clergy to bring us into relationship with God, we are to rely on ourselves—working together—to find God and the meaning he gives life. The doctrine of the universal priesthood of believers also enables Christian education through its implication that laypeople can and should teach others. Lay teaching is an essential ingredient of modern Christian education. Believer-priests are also to be servants, dedicated to spiritual renewal and to service of the Lord and his people. As priests and servants Christian educators should see their prime responsibility as helping others to find meaning in life and to become, in their own right, more effective priests and servants of the Most High God. As they do so, God's transforming grace will become ever more available to work its infinite power in the world.

3

Theology and Christian Education

Christian education needs theological grounding in the central doctrines of Christianity. However, it has become fashionable to downplay the connections between theology and Christian education. Some writers conceive of Christian education as an academic discipline in its own right that can contribute to theological inquiry as well as borrow from it. These authors are indeed right when they protest that religious education is much more than a handmaiden of theology (Lee 1973, p. 23). Christian education is not simply theological instruction for the laity, but education for Christian living. Christian education does more than simply transmit the latest findings of theologians and Bible scholars.

Many educators have reacted too strongly, however, and have failed to grasp the central role that theology inevitably possesses in Christian education. Theology is central not only because it is the content of Christian education (i.e., the stuff that is taught), but also because it most directly deals with the presuppositions lying behind Christian-education programs. As shown in chapter 2, certain theological beliefs provide the very foundation for Christian education as a discipline.

A distinction made by Nicholas Wolterstorff (1984) between "data beliefs" and "control beliefs" may be useful at this point to understand the role of theology in Christian education. Wolterstorff argues that the day-to-day work in any academic discipline of constructing and testing theories, developing paradigms, and identifying real-world implications is shaped not only by what we judge to be the relevant academic data (data beliefs), but by our other beliefs and values as well (control beliefs). These latter beliefs can be scientific theories, religious beliefs, superstitions, or any other vital part of a person's worldview. Control beliefs affect the shape of one's theories in any field of inquiry, but their influence is most profound in highly value-laden fields like education. Theological control-beliefs (e.g., beliefs about human nature or the attributes of God) affect one's conception of Christian education more than do the findings or methods of any other academic discipline. By definition one's theology will serve as the primary control-beliefs in any theorizing about Christian education.

It is difficult to identify indisputably the theological concepts that serve as control beliefs in shaping a person's theory of Christian education. However, several theological issues are frequently suggested as having a direct bearing. Every Christian educator will take at least an implicit stand on each of these issues. This can be said even of an educator who has not heard of a particular issue! For example, a person cannot undertake the task of Christian education without having answered the question, "What does it mean to know God?" The answer may never be articulated or systematized, but each person makes at least some sort of unconscious response that will direct his or her practice of Christian education.

This chapter examines five theological issues that have been prominent in debates about Christian education. They include knowledge of God, the purpose of the Bible, the role of the Holy Spirit, human nature, and Christian maturity. The positions taken on these issues give concrete shape and direction to educational ministry.

Knowledge of God

> What were we made for? To know God. What aim should
> we set ourselves in life? To know God. What is the "eternal
> life" that Jesus gives? Knowledge of God. "This is life eter-
> nal, that they might know thee, the only true God, and
> Jesus Christ, whom thou hast sent" (Jn 17:3). What is the
> best thing in life, bringing more joy, delight, and content-
> ment, than anything else? Knowledge of God. . . . What, of
> all the states God ever sees man in, gives Him most plea-
> sure? Knowledge of Himself. "I desire . . . the knowledge
> of God more than burnt offerings," says God (Hos 6:6).
> [Packer 1973, p. 29]

It has long been agreed that Christian education should
play a role in helping persons come to know God. Unfortunately, educators often disagree as to what it means to
promote the knowledge of God. Many of the divisions in
Christian education can be traced to this watershed issue.
Of course, the answer to this question is necessarily different for each religious group; consequently, I make no
pretense of offering an answer that all religious educators
can accept. My answer is rooted in the Hebraic conception of knowledge of God and in the New Testament
emphasis on spiritual regeneration as a prerequisite to
knowing God.

Knowledge as Relationship

The knowledge of God which concerns us here is not
an abstract knowledge learned solely from books and other
people, but the knowledge born of a mature relationship.
The closest parallel we experience to true knowledge of
God is the knowledge of another person which grows out
of a friendship. J. I. Packer put it well when he said, "Why
has God spoken? . . . The truly staggering answer which
the Bible gives to this question is that God's purpose in
revelation is to *make friends* with us" (1979, p. 50). God
desires a deep, loving friendship with each of us—a friendship in which each party comes to know and understand

the other. A marriage, a courtship, or a deep friendship cannot exist just on feelings. Coming to know the other person requires shared experiences, commitment, and communication.

A basic assumption in the field of communication is expressed by the formula "Communication = Content + Relationship" (Griffin 1982, p. 91). Any communication consists of the words which are said (content) and the thoughts and feelings which the people who are involved have about each other (relationship). The same words (e.g., "I love you") placed in different interpersonal contexts can have vastly different meanings. Knowledge of God or communication with him is dependent both on our grasping content (the Bible and theology) and on our experiencing a vital relationship with him. Without a reconciled relationship to God which is based on the work of Christ, true knowledge of God is impossible. And conversely, just as a relationship in which lovers or friends never exchange information about themselves is doomed, so too our relationship with God cannot develop merely on feelings of reconciliation. A growing friendship requires an objective understanding of what the other person is like (content).

The Insufficiency of Factual Knowledge

Many people believe that religious knowledge comes in two forms: "head knowledge" and "heart knowledge." Head knowledge (e.g., knowledge of theology or memorized Bible verses) is often seen as having only indirect impact upon one's religious life. Only when this information is internalized, or brought into one's heart, does it exercise consistent control in a person's life. By contrast, heart knowledge (i.e., one's values, beliefs, and attitudes) is said to be very important in a person's daily life. While this popular dichotomy has some limitations, it does point to one fundamental principle concerning Christian knowledge: knowing about God must never be confused with knowing God.

Words come very easily compared with corresponding deeds. James knew this truth very well and admonished his readers that it is deeds, not just beliefs and words, that ultimately count: "Show me your faith without deeds, and I will show you my faith by what I do. You believe that there is one God. Good! Even the demons believe that—and shudder" (James 2:18–19). The demons know about God, but they do not know God. The possession of certain beliefs or facts must not be equated with knowledge of God.

Old Testament prophets also made it very clear that many persons knew about God but at the same time were estranged from him. In the first chapter of Isaiah, Israel is described as not knowing the Lord:

> The ox knows his master,
> the donkey his owner's manger,
> but Israel does not know [me],
> my people do not understand.
>
> (v. 3)

Israel had not literally forgotten the name of Yahweh, for later in this chapter Isaiah mentions their God-directed prayers and sacrifices. Yet they lived their lives with little regard for the Holy One of Israel. They worshiped other gods and ignored Yahweh's commands. They knew of God's existence, but they did not know God. Regrettably, this problem is still present in the church. All too many ministers, theology professors, and Christian educators have a competent intellectual grasp of the Bible and doctrine, but show little evidence in their lives of having a close relationship with God.

The Insufficiency of Feelings

Reliance on heart knowledge, or knowledge based on feelings, was one of Israel's greatest problems. If the Hebrews *felt* that Baal, the Ashtaroth, or other competing religious systems would help produce crops, bring a victory, or cure an illness, they were quick to abandon the Lord. The message of Deuteronomy firmly opposed this tendency. Moses urged the Israelites to base their lives on God's character and not on their momentary feelings and experiences. They were to live lives consistent with the truth, "The LORD is our God, the LORD alone" (Deut. 6:4, margin). Perhaps the most memorable incident involving unwarranted reliance on feelings is the subject of a dramatic encounter between Samuel and Saul. King Saul had departed from God's explicit command about the disposal of booty because he was afraid of the people (1 Sam. 15:24); he apparently felt that his modification of God's command was perfectly acceptable. The Lord, however, brought a message of judgment through Samuel, who reminded Saul that "to obey is better than sacrifice" (v. 22). We might say today, To obey is better than doing what feels good.

In the New Testament, Paul considers the spiritual instability brought on by following one's momentary feelings to be a mark of immaturity. He desires that the Ephesians "no longer be infants, tossed back and forth by the waves, and blown here and there by every wind of teaching and by the cunning and craftiness of men in their deceitful scheming" (Eph. 4:14). Paul wants the Ephesians to manifest the stability that comes only by using something more permanent than feelings as a guide for life. Knowledge of and relationship with God are to be based on something more than mere feelings.

The issue of feeling-based and cognitive knowing must be addressed because so many religious educators have chosen to emphasize feelings almost to the exclusion of cognitive knowledge. There is a pervasive sense in both liberal and conservative Christian education that we must be far more concerned about feelings than about knowledge. In actuality, many Christian educators are not so much feeling-oriented as they are noncognitive or anticognitive in their educational approach. A summary of a six-step lesson plan found in a nationally distributed teaching guide will serve as an illustration (Griggs 1977, pp. 21–23):

1. Ask the students to relate some of the ideas they used to have about God.
2. Read Psalm 95:1–7 and discuss it.
3. "Focus on hands." One suggestion: "Have each person look at his/her own hands, then respond spontaneously as a group" to questions like, "What would it be like to be without hands?" Another suggestion: "Look through magazines to find pictures of hands expressing feelings and actions of hands. Make individual or group montages."
4. Have the group form a circle and hold hands, then sing "He's Got the Whole World in His Hands." Lest there be any doubt what the curriculum writer is after, he adds, "With the group in a circle holding hands or possibly putting hands and arms around each other's shoulders or waists, the feeling of closeness is communicated. Our hands bring us closer to each other."
5. Read a poem about hands. Then instruct the students, "Go to the table where there is clay. Play and create with the clay in any way that expresses your feelings in response to what we have done or to the poem."
6. After the students have spent fifteen to twenty minutes with the clay, conclude the session by asking, "What have you learned about Psalm 95?"

Numerous examples of similarly noncognitive Christian-education materials could be found from virtually any theological orientation. Such curricula are a matter for concern, not because of their aim to be holistic or to include the feeling, or affective, dimension in the teaching process, but because of their anticognitive stance; they almost glorify the nonrational element. Many people, however, find education that is oriented around feelings to be trite and cute, and far from providing the deep and moving experience its well-intentioned designers desire.

I have experienced two approaches to teaching Ecclesiastes to adult Sunday-school classes. One teacher had a decidedly experiential orientation. He had the class mold Styrofoam cups into shapes that reflected "the condition of our lives" and announced that he would take us "through the back door"—presumably a noncognitive entrance—into Ecclesiastes. The teacher talked about how difficult life is and evidently cared deeply about people, but not many of the class members felt they had understood Ecclesiastes. The other class looked at Ecclesiastes from a literary perspective. The students read the text carefully, thought long and hard about its meaning, and viewed slides that contemporized the images in the book. Through the talents of a good teacher, the message of the book was both understood and deeply felt. The first class ended with some good laughs, some self-disclosure, and much bewilderment about Ecclesiastes. The second class left with a grasp of the book, a sense of wonder, and regret that the period of shared enrichment was over.

Experientially oriented educators mistakenly assert that our depth of feeling about something increases as our understanding decreases. They are wrong. Beauty, mystery, appreciation, attraction, and awe are usually built on a thoughtful understanding. Head knowledge and heart knowledge are not contradictory alternatives. In fact, neither of them in isolation represents the biblical conception of religious knowledge.

True Knowledge of God:
Facts, Feelings, and Proper Relationship

For the Hebrews, knowledge of God meant "recognition of, and obedience to, one who acted purposefully in the world" (Blackman 1950, p. 121). To know something meant to have experienced it or observed it in such a way that it made an impact on one's life. Thus the statement that Christ "knew no sin" (2 Cor. 5:21, RSV) does not mean that he had no intellectual comprehension of sin, but rather that he had never personally experienced sin. The Hebraic notion that knowledge entails a personal relationship or involvement can be seen in the biblical use of "know" to describe sexual relations: "Now Adam knew Eve his wife, and she conceived and bore Cain" (Gen. 4:1, RSV). Something is known when it becomes a part of one, not simply when it can be defined or recognized.

From a biblical perspective, knowledge is both the result of a relationship with God and one of the major factors that strengthens our relationship with him. It is both the product and catalyst of this relationship. Factual knowledge and feeling-based knowledge must be coupled with an experiential knowledge of God. Persons can know God only if they have walked with him, worshiped him, prayed to him—in other words, lived as if his existence mattered. This is not to diminish the value of the Bible in the process of coming to know God, for the Bible is a necessary and irreplaceable source of information about God. Knowledge of the Bible, however, must always be seen as a means to an end, namely, knowledge of God, which can come only through the work of Jesus Christ. Christian education is hollow and meaningless unless educators acknowledge—both implicitly and explicitly—the importance of knowing God deeply and personally. No amount of activity can compensate for an educator's own inability to relate to God or to communicate the importance of that relationship.

The Purpose of the Bible

In the early nineteenth century the Bible was widely adopted as the basic content of Sunday-school curricula in the United States. This step represented a move away from catechisms and was undertaken in part as a response to the theological pluralism which prevailed throughout the land. Immigration, revivals, and religious freedom produced a nation made up of a variety of denominations. The theological diversity present even within evangelical American Christianity (e.g., Baptists, Methodists, Presbyterians, and Congregationalists) proved to be a real challenge to early Christian educational work.

In the early 1830s the American Sunday School Union embarked upon an ambitious missionary project to plant a Sunday school in "every destitute place in the Mississippi Valley." In this campaign the union had to face squarely the challenge of theological diversity. The union's strategy was to establish in each village a single Sunday school which would serve all the children of the community irrespective of denomination. This cooperative strategy compelled the union to provide materials and to conduct classes in a thoroughly nondenominational fashion. It became obvious that traditional Sunday-school materials like the Westminster Catechism were too narrow and doctrinaire to work in such a setting, and the last thing the American Sunday School Union wanted to do was offend any part of its constituency. The union's concern to teach only the essentials of the faith was evident in one of the annual reports: "It is known that among the members of our association are Baptists, Methodists, Presbyterians, Episcopalians, and others; and it is understood between us all, that our library books, manuals of instruction and whatever other agency we may employ, shall not, in any wise, inculcate opinions, or teach doctrines about which those various bodies of Christians are not agreed" (1833, p. 14). Union missionaries realized that children in a cooperative Sunday school could all agree that King David was a good man, whereas they might not agree on the answer to the catechism's question, "What is effectual calling?" The Bible was initially adopted as the primary content of Christian education in America because it rep-

resented the least common denominator (Wilhoit 1983a).
On Bible stories there was little disagreement. "Theology
divides, the Bible unites!" could well have been the slogan
of the day.

The social and theological context of Christian education in America has changed dramatically from the days
of the frontier missionaries. Today Christian education
takes place primarily within the context of, or at least in
relationship to, a local church that is part of a denomination. Cooperative Sunday schools are largely a relic of
the past, but the union's solution to the unique problem
posed by these schools can be seen in contemporary Christian-education curricula, especially among evangelicals.
We have inherited from our nineteenth-century forebears
a tendency to avoid serious grappling with the biblical text
for fear of being divisive. We have chosen the easier alternative of simply teaching names, places, and other facts.

While the Bible will always be a common ground for all
true Christians, we should teach it not because we see it
as a relatively noncontroversial book, but because we know
that it promotes Christian maturity. It cannot do so, however, unless we go beneath the surface level and begin to
apply Scripture to our personal situations.

The Bible as Subject Matter

The educational process contains essentially four major
elements: subject matter, student, teacher, and environment. These four elements interrelate dynamically as
shown in figure 1. A teacher cannot simply teach junior-
high-school students; they must be taught *something.*
Likewise, one cannot simply teach the Bible; it must be
taught to *someone.* The Bible is always taught in a specific
social and physical environment and to a unique audience.
A good instructor recognizes the unique situation that
each teaching opportunity provides and then teaches accordingly. As we consider the Bible as the subject matter

Figure 1 **Essential Elements in the Educational Process**

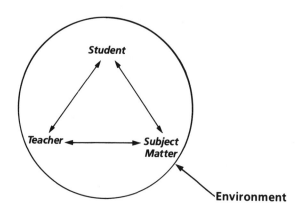

of Christian education, we must not forget the importance of the other elements in the teaching and learning process.

There are two major views of the Bible as subject matter. In the first, the subject matter is a *product* which needs to be delivered. The teacher is likened to the driver of a delivery truck who drops off needed products to various customers. The teacher delivers needed information to the students and, like the truck driver, moves on when sure that the knowledge has been properly delivered. The teacher's concern is with good communication and delivery, not with what the pupil does with the knowledge. Many of the teachers who subscribe to this view believe that knowledge of the Bible will inevitably lead to the presence of Christian graces. Others believe that the Holy Spirit is needed to apply the biblical knowledge to the pupil's life.

The second view considers the subject matter of the Bible as a *vehicle* (Soltis 1978). The instructor teaches the Bible to a student so that something else will occur. The teacher always aims at a goal which is beyond the immediate transmission of information. Teaching the Bible becomes, then, a means to an end and not an end in itself. The Bible is the indispensable guide used on one's pilgrimage to maturity and holiness. God desires that our lives be marked with love for him and service of our fellow humans, not just that our minds be filled with Bible facts.

The difference between these two perspectives is profound. Both honor the Bible, but the former sees Bible instruction as an end in and of itself, while the latter correctly views Bible instruction as a means to promoting fellowship with God. Consider again Packer's assessment of why God has spoken:

> Why has God spoken? ... The truly staggering answer which the Bible gives to this question is that God's purpose in revelation is to *make friends* with us. It was to this end that He created us rational beings, bearing His image, able to think and hear and speak and love; He wanted there to be genuine personal affection and friendship, two-sided, between Himself and us—a relation, not like that between a man and his dog, but like that of a father to his son, or a husband to his wife. Loving friendship between two persons has no ulterior motive; it is an end in itself. And this is God's end in revelation. He speaks to us simply to fulfill the purpose for which we were made; that is, to bring into being a relationship in which He is a friend to us, and we to Him, He finding His joy in giving us gifts and we finding ours in giving Him thanks. [1979, p. 50]

In other words, we should teach the Bible in order to introduce people to God and to strengthen their relationship with him. Bible facts are useful to the extent that they help us come to know God more fully.

The Bible as Spiritual Tool

The Bible was intended by God to serve as a spiritual tool (2 Tim. 3:16). It was designed to be used, not just displayed or studied. When the Bible is seen as a vehicle, a spiritual tool, or a source of spiritual nourishment, we are reminded that teaching the Bible is only a first step in Christian education. This view does not downplay Bible content, for "nothing will take the place of sound doctrine and the facts of the Word of God. But it is possible to starve people with Biblical facts, to make doctrine a substitute for spiritual reality, to fail our people by denying them the intimate personal experience with the Lord Himself who alone will satisfy the deepest longings of the human heart" (LeBar 1981, p. 18).

The Bible rightly plays a central role in Christian education because it is God's instrument for promoting spiritual growth and fellowship with him. According to Randolph Crump Miller, "The task of Christian education is not to teach theology, but to use theology as the basic tool for bringing learners into the right relationship with God" (1950, p. 6). Calling the Bible a spiritual tool is not to depersonalize it nor to diminish its uniqueness, but to focus on several of its most significant purposes:

To help people become friends with God.

To serve as the map for each Christian's pilgrimage.

To serve as a blueprint for the church.

To provide spiritual refreshment and nourishment.

To transform one's mind, habits, and patterns of living.

To challenge our small ideas of who God is and what he desires from us.

To provide a common language and norm for our public worship.

To define God's plan for meaning and purpose in life.

Of course, one danger of viewing the Bible as a tool is that we may wrongly conclude that we have the power and right to use it as we wish. Humility is certainly needed here, for only God can bring spiritual insight and growth. In the final analysis, "the Bible is not so much a book [nor a tool] as a place, the place where the human soul has its rendezvous with God" (Niles 1958, p. 51).

The Bible and Life

Christian educators do well when they strive to develop Bible-centered Christian-education materials. In addition to containing God's instructions for life and practice, the Bible serves as a refreshing and revitalizing means of grace. No ordinary human book, it must be accorded a primary place in Christian education. However, being Bible-centered is not enough. Effective Christian educators not only are concerned that the Bible is used, but care deeply about *how* it is used. The Bible contains God's words, but it is not a magical book which transforms people regardless of who teaches it or how it is taught. What counts in Christian education is that the Bible be handled in such a way that God's grace clearly shines through the teaching and that its meaning is related directly to the lives of the students.

Clear educational implications are packed into the affirmation that the Bible is both a means of grace and a guide for life. The teacher must both handle the Bible as a channel for God's renewing grace to the class members and relate it to their life situations. The teacher is not simply giving rules from God, but serving divine food. An effective Bible teacher does not merely transmit facts about God, but moves students to refresh themselves by washing their souls in the Word of God. Effective Bible teaching refreshes, renews, cleanses, and illuminates as much as it informs, convicts, and inspires.

Since we see the Bible as a map for righteous living, our teaching needs to emphasize both the content of Scripture and concrete life situations. The debates that have dogged Christian education in the twentieth century between those who advocate a Bible-centered approach and those who call for a life-centered approach have often

FIGURE 2   **A Bible- and Life-Centered Approach**

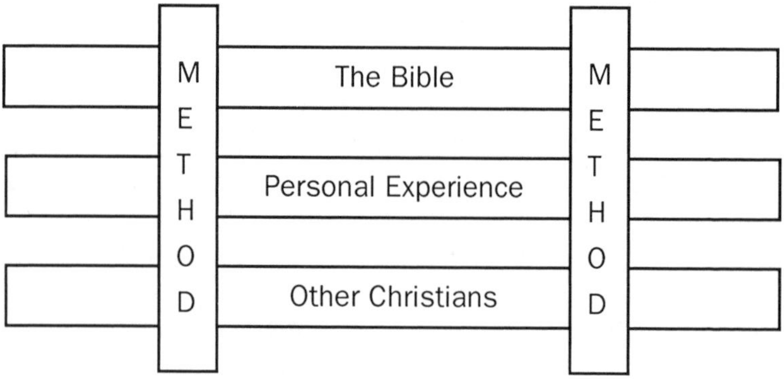

M E T H O D	The Bible	M E T H O D
	Personal Experience	
	Other Christians	

From *Pilgrims in Progress,* © 1990 by Jim and Carol Plueddemann. Used by permission of Harold Shaw Publishers, Wheaton, Ill.

led to deformed curricula when educators choose one pole over the other. Effective Christian education will never be exclusively Bible-centered or life-centered. It may be helpful to conceive of an effective approach as entailing three prominent elements: (1) the teaching of the Bible; (2) a study of our own lives; and (3) lessons from the lives of other Christians. This can be viewed schematically as a fence (Ward and Rowen 1972; Plueddemann and Plueddemann 1990). The top rail in figure 2 represents study and teaching of the Bible, while the bottom two rails represent study of our own personal experience and that of other Christians. The three rails are joined together by various teaching methods. For example, a class may pray for God to apply a particular passage of Scripture to their lives. At other times a teacher's pointed questions or class discussions may lead to consideration of how the Bible affects one's personal experience. While the methods will vary, what is vitally important is that both the Bible and life be studied in our classes and tied together. All too often, classes either study the Bible or simply share about life without bringing to their own particular situations any biblical reflection.

The Role of the Holy Spirit

There is little dispute today that the Holy Spirit is involved in the Christian-education process. However, educators do not fully agree concerning the nature of the Spirit's work in Christian teaching and learning. To some, the presence of the Holy Spirit minimizes or even eliminates the need for a teacher; to others, the Holy Spirit is concerned primarily with applying the Bible lesson to the student's life. Each of these views has at least some scriptural support. A well-developed theology of the Holy Spirit's role in Christian education, however, must be based on all the relevant biblical passages and themes, and not on just a few of special interest.

Incomplete Views of the Spirit's Work

Identifying the Holy Spirit's role in Christian education will be made easier if some of the current inadequate views can first be set aside. These views are faulty in that they have focused on one aspect of the Spirit's work to the exclusion of other important aspects.

One of the inadequate views of the Holy Spirit's task is that he merely delivers the content (i.e., the material being studied) to the student. It is maintained that in a Christian-education setting the Holy Spirit's prime role is efficient transmittal of the biblical content from the teacher to the student. By extension some writers claim that the Holy Spirit will work in the same way for the Christian student in a secular setting (e.g., he will convey a knowledge of calculus to a Christian student at a state university). Unfortunately for this view, we have no proof that Christian students do better than their non-Christian classmates. The major problem with this understanding of the Holy Spirit is that it commands virtually no biblical support and often trivializes the Spirit's task.

The Holy Spirit is described as bringing to remembrance Christ's words (John 14:26), guiding us into an understanding of the truth (John 16:13), and illuminating the revelation God has given us (1 Cor. 2:12–16), to name just a few of the Spirit's activities. However, there are few references to his being the deliverer of content. It must be granted that conviction by the Holy Spirit often involves not only insight, but a forceful presentation of God's truth as well. The problem with the view that the Holy Spirit's basic role in Christian education is to deliver content is that it focuses exclusively on what the Bible sees as only a relatively minor part of the Spirit's work.

Another popular view is that the Holy Spirit's sole work in Christian education is to apply the biblical lesson to life. One form of this position maintains that *only* the Holy Spirit can implement a teaching in the student's life. Consequently, the teacher is urged to teach well and then let the Holy Spirit take over. Teaching the content is seen as primarily a human activity, and applying it is thought to be largely a divine work. So the teacher is to teach well and then "let go and let God" take over.

Leaving it up to the Holy Spirit alone to apply the lesson was not a mark of either Jesus' or Paul's ministry. In bidding farewell to the Ephesian elders Paul reminded them, "For three years I never stopped warning each of you night and day with tears" (Acts 20:31). In spite of the Holy Spirit's profoundly important role in application, Paul did not abandon his own responsibility to admonish, support, teach, and pray for the Ephesians. There is no evidence that Paul and Jesus diminished their efforts because they expected the Holy Spirit to take up the slack.

A more radical view holds that human teachers are not needed to instruct Spirit-filled Christians, that the Holy Spirit is the only teacher a sincere Christian needs. This view is inevitably based in part on 1 John 2:27, which states, "The anointing you received from him remains in you, and you do not need anyone to teach you." Taken in isolation, this verse indeed seems to minimize the Christian's need to be taught by others. This interpretation,

however, conflicts with other portions of Scripture, spe-
cifically those dealing with the gift of teaching which
Christ bestowed on his church, the ministry of the apos-
tles, and the characteristics of a sound teaching ministry
(see, e.g., 2 Tim.).

To understand precisely what John is saying in 1 John
2:27, we must consider that part of his purpose in writing
was to combat the Gnostic heresy, which asserted that
the "unenlightened" Christians to whom John was writing were without salvation because they did not know the
secret oracles. John denied this Gnostic claim and told the
Christians that there was no hidden knowledge; they already knew everything they needed to know for their salvation. That he did not mean to say that there is no need
for human teachers is evident from the fact that he himself
was teaching through his letter. Although John emphasized the role of the Spirit in leading Christians to truth,
it is clear from the Bible as a whole that believers are not
to rely only on the Spirit for instruction.

Dimensions of the Spirit's Work

In figure 1 (p. 46) four aspects of the educational process
were identified: teacher, student, subject matter, and environment. These four elements of teaching will be used
here as a framework for exploring a more balanced view of
the Spirit's work in Christian education.

1. *The Spirit and the teacher.* The Holy Spirit acts in
several ways to facilitate the work of the teacher. First,
the Spirit graciously gives certain persons the gift of teaching (Rom. 12:7). Through inborn endowments or direct
intervention, the Holy Spirit has equipped certain Christians with the ability and desire to teach others. This gift
includes spiritual insight (1 Cor. 12:8, 10), motivation to
minister (2 Tim. 1:6–7), and the ability to communicate
effectively (2 Tim. 2:24).

Second, the Holy Spirit gradually remakes Christians—
both teachers and students—from the inside out. The full-

ness of the image of God is being restored as Christians open themselves to the working of God's grace: "And we, who with unveiled faces all reflect the Lord's glory, are being transformed into his likeness with ever-increasing glory, which comes from the Lord, who is the Spirit" (2 Cor. 3:18). This process of transformation is not automatic; it occurs to the degree that Christians present their "bodies as living sacrifices, holy and pleasing to God." He commands, "Do not conform any longer to the pattern of this world, but be transformed by the renewing of your mind" (Rom. 12:1–2). The Holy Spirit is working to produce love, joy, peace, patience, kindness, goodness, faithfulness, gentleness, and self-control (Gal. 5:22–23) in the life of the Christian who depends upon him. In this process of spiritual renewal the Holy Spirit is making the Christian teacher a better teacher. And what teacher is there who does not need more patience or kindness or love for his or her pupils? The Holy Spirit is at work to deepen the Christian teacher's spiritual insight, compassion, and goodness. Those characteristics which are often listed as the marks of a good teacher—enthusiasm, warmth, and acceptance—are but pale shadows of the fruit of the Spirit. The fruit of the Spirit comprises attributes (love, joy, self-control, etc.) which might well be called the marks of a great teacher.

In Christian education, the character of the teacher is as important as the knowledge the teacher has. Jesus clearly taught this concept when he said, "A student is not above his teacher, but everyone who is fully trained will be like his teacher" (Luke 6:40). It follows that students will seldom rise above the spiritual maturity of their teacher. Teaching is not just a matter of technique and knowledge. One's character and interests are vitally involved in the process of Christian instruction, so teachers need to open themselves to the Spirit's renewing power. Otherwise they may well function as a barrier to their students' growth in personal spirituality and in knowledge of and love for the Lord.

Third, a significant ministry of the Holy Spirit in the lives of Christians is illumination. This ministry is of special importance to Christian teachers, since it enables them to comprehend and appreciate Christian truths. Various passages depict the illuminating role of the Holy Spirit:

> We have not received the spirit of the world but the Spirit who is from God, that we may understand what God has freely given us. . . . The man without the Spirit does not accept the things that come from the Spirit of God, for they are foolishness to him, and he cannot understand them, because they are spiritually discerned. [1 Cor. 2:12, 14]

> For God, who said, "Let light shine out of darkness," made his light shine in our hearts to give us the light of the knowledge of the glory of God in the face of Christ. [2 Cor. 4:6]

> I pray also that the eyes of your heart may be enlightened in order that you may know the hope to which he has called you, the riches of his glorious inheritance in the saints, and his incomparably great power for us who believe. [Eph. 1:18–19]

The Spirit illuminates the teacher in two ways. First, the Holy Spirit gives the Christian spiritual sight. Since the fall, humankind has suffered from poor spiritual vision; Paul declared that "the god of this age has blinded the minds of unbelievers, so that they cannot see the light of the gospel of the glory of Christ, who is the image of God" (2 Cor. 4:4). Unbelievers are blinded to the truth found in God's revelation. Roy Zuck comments on this phenomenon of spiritual blindness: "God's word is not in any way defective or insufficient. The fault lies with man. It is as though a blind man were facing the sun. The fault that he cannot see the light is not the fault of the sun; the deficiency lies with him" (1972, p. 51). The Holy Spirit provides Christians with spiritual vision so that they can see the significance of God's revelation. Without such illumination Christians would continue to be "darkened in their understanding . . . having lost all sensitivity" to God's message (Eph. 4:18–19).

The spiritual vision provided by the Holy Spirit enables believers to *perceive* the truth of revelation, while his quickening enables them to *receive* that truth warmly. Of course, persons alienated from God are able to study and understand the objective meaning of Scripture to some degree. Non-Christians have made positive contributions to biblical scholarship. However, only the spiritually renewed will readily welcome the message of God's revelation. Zuck summarizes this twofold aspect of illumination: "Illumination is the Spirit's work, enabling Christians to discern the meaning of the message and to welcome and receive it as from God" (1972, p. 54). The Holy Spirit works in the life of the Christian teacher by bestowing the gift of teaching, by renewing the teacher's character, and by illuminating the Word of God.

2. *The Spirit and the student.* The Holy Spirit is active in the lives of both the student and the teacher in several parallel ways. In both, the Spirit brings spiritual birth, spiritual vision, and spiritual receptivity. Of particular relevance to the Christian-education process is the Spirit's ministry of indwelling. Through this ministry the students receive a new spirituality, a new motivation to study spiritual things. The spirituality brought about by the indwelling of the Holy Spirit must be nurtured, for it is this fundamental change wrought by the Spirit that makes Christian education possible. As John Calvin reminds us, "Paul so highly commends the 'ministry of the Spirit' [II Cor. 3:6] for the reason that teachers would shout to no effect if Christ himself, inner Schoolmaster, did not by his Spirit draw to himself those given to him by the Father" (1960, 3.1.4). In addition, the Holy Spirit convicts and guides students about areas in their lives which need attention.

In previous decades motivation was portrayed as the key variable that determines whether something is learned or not. This conclusion is now questioned, but motivation is still regarded as an important variable in the teaching and learning process. The highly motivated learner can master subjects that might otherwise seem far too advanced. Teachers in elementary schools "regularly see the 'pterodactyl phenomenon' as seven- and eight-year-olds successfully struggle with a reference book on prehistoric animals" (Harrison 1980, p. 13); not surprisingly, students find pterodactyls far more interesting than the adventures of Dick and Jane.

Motivation is important in the process of Christian growth. We tend to study with eagerness what we find meaningful or interesting. In this regard the Holy Spirit can be of immense help to the student—the Spirit can engender an interest in the spiritual dimension of life. A desire for Bible study, prayer, and spiritual disciplines can be instilled by the Spirit. However, he does not automatically induce such motivation in all believers. Personal diligence in study is often a prerequisite to the Spirit's ministry of renewal.

Another work of the Holy Spirit in the lives of students is to give them a desire for service. Active service will in turn be yet another inducement to learning, for it will fill them with questions and concerns. Douglas Hyde in his book *Dedication and Leadership* has described how the Communists effectively use party service as a way of generating interest in learning. A new convert, for example, was not immediately put into classes to learn about communism, but assigned to a street corner. As he sold Communist papers and pamphlets, he was asked questions about the Soviet Union and communism which he could not adequately answer. Inevitably this green recruit found his defense of communism to be less convincing to the passersby than he had imagined. He left his curbside propaganda work with a thirst to learn so that he would serve the cause better the next time he had the opportunity. Hyde comments:

Those who sent him into this form of activity did not
expect him to have all the answers. He has let down neither the Party nor himself. In the process he has learned
a good deal. When he next takes up his stand at the side
of the road, he will come determined to do better. Most
probably, he has been reading Communist papers in a different way, looking for the answers to the questions he was
asked last time. Gathering shot and shell in readiness for
the next fight. This is when he really begins to learn—and
the desire to learn now comes from within himself. [1966,
pp. 44–45]

Service predisposes a person to learn. As Hyde docu-
ments, the Communists at times seem to have understood
this truth better than the church has. It is highly significant for Christian education that each believer is equipped
by the Holy Spirit with a spiritual gift for serving others.
Utilizing this gift in Christian service will help show believers their limitations, and in their Spirit-born desire to
serve more effectively, they will become eager learners.

3. *The Spirit and subject matter.* The primary content
of Christian education is the Bible, but Christian education consists of more than just Bible teaching. "Christian
education must be concerned not about the Bible alone,
but about the whole of life with which the Bible deals.
The scope of Christian education is the whole gospel and
the whole of life in the light of the gospel" (Henderlite
1964, p. 117).

The Bible was born through the work of the Holy Spirit.
Through the inspiration of the Spirit, the writers were able
to give divine interpretations to the acts of God they wit-
nessed. Consider Christ's crucifixion. To a passerby it
may have looked like an ordinary execution, an all-too-
common event in first-century Palestine. However, to the
Spirit-directed Gospel writer, it was a turning point in
"His-story," the provision of humanity with redemption.
Interpreting God's actions, speaking his message, and giving hope to a troubled nation and world—the prophets did

all of this through the power of the Spirit. Without the Spirit there would not be a Bible, and without the Spirit today the Bible would hardly be God's Word for his church. The Spirit enlivens his people and his book so that we can hear the Word of God.

The Spirit has not abandoned the Bible today. He still works through it to speak God's Word to the church and the world. In fact, reading, studying, and hearing the Bible preached are means of God's grace largely because they expose us to the Spirit's power, presence, and work. In at least three concrete ways the Holy Spirit illumines and empowers the Scriptures (Henderlite 1964, pp. 62–63).

First, the Spirit testifies that the Bible is the Word of God. This is not to say that there are not good and sufficient objective evidences for the divine nature of the Bible. But it is by the Spirit working with and through these evidences and the personal experiences of the believer that the Christian becomes firmly convinced of the Bible's divine nature. The Westminster Confession gives prominence to the Spirit's role in convincing us of the Bible's origins and authority: "We may be moved and induced by the testimony of the Church to an high and reverent esteem of the Holy Scripture. . . . Yet, notwithstanding, our full persuasion and assurance of the infallible truth, and divine authority thereof, is from the inward work of the Holy Spirit, bearing witness by and with the Word in our hearts" (1.5).

Second, the Holy Spirit uses Scripture to witness to and glorify Jesus Christ. Jesus declared of the coming Spirit, "He will bring glory to me by taking from what is mine and making it known to you" (John 16:14). The Spirit directs us to the central person of the Scriptures—Jesus Christ. Through this leading we meet not only the historic Jesus of the first century, but the living Word of God.

Finally, the Holy Spirit acts to give contemporary significance to the message and events of the Bible. To the Spirit-directed Christian the pages of the Bible become personally relevant. Søren Kierkegaard used the analogy of a love letter to describe the pertinence the Bible has for Christians: "Think of a lover who has now received a letter from his beloved—as precious as this letter is to the lover, just so precious to thee, I assume, is God's Word" (1941, p. 51).

4. *The Spirit and the environment.* Christian education takes place in the church, an environment charged with the power of the Spirit. And he continues to work at transforming his people and the church into the likeness of Christ. Whether it be the church gathered in corporate worship or the church scattered in witness and various vocations, the Holy Spirit can be present in his fullness to radically alter the spiritual environment. We say "can" because there is the possibility that his ministry will be thwarted by spiritual lethargy or hardness on the part of God's people.

Generally, the educational environment is considered a given, something the teacher is stuck with or blessed with. Teachers acknowledge its presence and hope that it will foster constructive attitudes. However, from a Christian educator's standpoint, the Spirit's work in the church creates a positive educational environment. Because the Holy Spirit is at work transforming the church, the church should be a good place to learn.

Christian education is concerned with promoting learning in tough, hard-to-change areas, crusty old habits and ways of viewing the world. The supportive environment of the church, where the committed people of God show love to one another, is an ideal place to question and change non-Christian values acquired from the secular culture. Paul points out that the gifts of the Spirit to the church, which include pastors and teachers, are intended to build up those who stand in need of spiritual growth: these gifts "prepare God's people for works of service, so that the body of Christ may be built up until we all reach unity in the faith and in the knowledge of the Son of God and become mature, attaining to the whole measure of the fullness of Christ" (Eph. 4:12–13). The Holy Spirit, the transformer of the church, works to make it the kind of community where people can rid themselves of their enslaving habits, their crushing doubts, and their nagging worries. In New Testament terms, it provides a place where believers can change into spiritual clothes: "What you learned was to fling off the dirty clothes of the old way of living, which were rotted through and through with lust's illusions, and, with yourselves mentally and spiritually remade, to put on the clean fresh clothes of the new life which was made by God's design for righteousness and the holiness which is no illusion" (Eph. 4:22–24, Phillips).

The Spirit blows where he will (John 3:8). He is not capricious, but neither can he be programed. Yet through prayer and humility he can be brought into Christian education, where his presence is necessary. We must approach him gently, as one would approach a dove so as not to frighten it away, but at the same time we must also respect him greatly, acknowledging that his is the hand that formed the world we live in.

Human Nature

Grandeur and Misery

The biblical view of human nature runs counter to contemporary approaches to education. The Bible calls us to acknowledge the "grandeur as well as the misery of man" (Bloesch 1979, p. 88). In the biblical view, people are made in the image of God, yet they are sinners. They are capable of great self-sacrifice for others, and yet, apart from Christ, they are unable to please God fully. This view of human nature has no parallel in secular theories of education and is the main obstacle to the Christian's adopting any such theory wholesale. The romantic position that the child is fundamentally good and the radical behaviorist notion that persons are to be viewed as machines simply do not square with the biblical witness. Grandeur and fallenness, sinner and yet bearer of God's image—these are the tensions with which education that is truly Christian must deal.

Evangelicals often seem to be far more pessimistic about the human situation than the biblical account would warrant. Despite our fallenness we are capable, with God's help, of leading lives of remarkable holiness and dedication. David was "a man after [God's] own heart" (1 Sam. 13:14), which reminds us that God can take true delight in his creation. In Revelation 2–3, Christ addresses letters to seven churches in Asia Minor. In his letters, four of the seven churches receive mixed reviews (e.g., "I know your deeds, your love and faith. . . . Nevertheless, I have this against you . . ." [2:19–20]); and one church, Laodicea, receives all bad marks. However, two churches, Smyrna and Philadelphia, receive only words of encouragement and commendation from Christ. It is possible, then, for a properly ordered human institution to please God. Christians must never think of the fallenness of humankind as obliterating their more distinctive mark—the image of God, which is marred but never fully erased. Christ, who was fully human, was also perfectly good. And through God's grace human beings can live lives of immense creativity, harmony, and service, both individually and corporately.

The Effects of Sin and the Need for Conversion

Sin is the aspect of human nature which calls for our attention here. Sin is endemic to the human race, but it does not affect all persons and all cultures equally. Children, for example, usually do not feel the hardening and limiting effects of sin in the same way adults do. The romantic notion that children simply need to discover their harmony with God enjoys no biblical support, but neither does the conversionist position that Christian education must be exclusively evangelistic until a child has made a verbal and datable confession of faith in Jesus

Christ. Children differ from adults, not because a primordial innocence still clings to them, but because sin has not hardened them in the same way it has hardened adults.

All persons are sinners separated from God and standing in need of reconciliation. However, the condition of the young child of believing and faithful parents is vastly different from that of the middle-aged man who has overtly rejected the gospel numerous times. Such an adult has developed patterns of rejection that predispose him to reject any further presentation of the gospel. The Bible uses the metaphors of having a "heart of stone" (Ezek. 11:19) and of being "stiff-necked" (Deut. 10:16) to describe the cumulative effects of sin upon the individual.

The cumulative effect of our individual actions is a theme that runs through the writings of C. S. Lewis. In *The Great Divorce* (1946), Lewis describes a bus trip from hell to heaven. All the riders have the option of not returning to hell, but only one chooses to stay in heaven and enjoy its delights. This person was formerly trapped by lust, a sin which Lewis thought was far easier to escape from than habitual acts of pride. The others return to the dismal bus because, hardened and blinded as they are by repeated individual acts of pride, they are unable to see heaven's beauty.

Lewis has identified a key aspect of human nature that bears upon our spiritual life. Every day we strengthen our habits of holiness and habits of ungodliness. The simple choice of pausing in the morning to pray increases, ever so slightly, the likelihood that one will stop to pray the next day. Similarly, speaking a kind and gentle word in a difficult situation makes one more likely to do the same in another trying circumstance. Habits are not broken or set permanently aside in one decisive act of the will; habits tend to stick around. This fact has some positive implications; for example, habits of punctuality or courtesy do not disappear the first time a punctual person is late or a courteous person is ungracious. Winston Churchill observed that "we shape our buildings: thereafter they shape us." Much the same could be said for habits: we shape our habits; thereafter they shape us. We are not hopelessly trapped by our habits, but changing them is usually a slow process and can ultimately be accomplished only as we open ourselves to the working of God's grace. Mark Twain commented wisely, "Habit is habit, and not to be flung out the window by any man, but coaxed downstairs a step at a time." To the Christian the Holy Spirit gives the grace to set aside imprisoning habits gradually and to adopt new habits of holiness and love.

The possibility of gradual reform in no way displaces the need for conversion. Dramatic conversions do occur and are necessary for many individuals. The New Testament emphasis on conversion was shaped by the missionary outreach to Gentile adults who had experienced the hardening effects of sin and had to be called to repentance. A hardened adult cannot be simply nurtured into the faith; a radical casting off of the old life through repentance is needed. William James and many psychologists today speak of the importance of making a clean, dramatic break with a lifestyle and belief system that have become unbearable. For persons mired deeply in a life far removed from God, gradual reform is highly unlikely.

There is no biblical warrant for trying to convert the children of Christian parents in the same way that we attempt to convert adults. Yet Christian education of children must not adopt an insipid "Jesus wants me for a sunbeam" orientation that denies the reality of sin in human life and the demands of the gospel. Church-education programs for children should stress the nurturing of their faith through age-appropriate discipleship. Although he was unorthodox in his theology, Horace Bushnell was quite insightful when he said, "The child is to grow up a Christian, and never know himself as being otherwise" (1979, p. 10). Thus children need not experience a datable conversion, but they must come to understand the joy of living in fellowship with God as well as the agony and aimlessness that they would have outside of Christ.

Of course, we must be wary of the notion that one can evolve into a Christian. The image of the new birth depicts radical change, a complete metamorphosis, but it need not be *sudden* change. Conception, pregnancy, and birth are a process which takes place over a period of time and includes numerous small crises. The nurturing of children is not a process of spiritual evolution but of guiding them through their spiritual birth. When they look back, they will know that they were spiritually born, though they may not be able to name a specific date of birth.

Reasons for Failure in Christian Education

Americans put great stock in the power of education to change society and eliminate a multitude of social ills from teenage pregnancy to racial prejudice. This belief has rubbed off on American churches, many of which have taken Bushnell's words to heart and blithely assumed that good Christian-education programs cannot fail to mold perfect Christians. The Christian educator must be careful, however, not to assign too much transforming power to religious education. *History has shown that education alone cannot spiritually revive a nation or a church.* We may wish that schooling could guarantee renewed spirits and enlightened personal ethics, but it cannot. Since education depends on the individual's cooperation and involves personal choice, it will never achieve total compliance.

The church will not be reformed or transformed by adult education no matter what its exponents claim or expect. . . . The church is destructively, perversely, tragically, malignantly, willfully ignorant. Such ignorance, because it is willful, cannot be touched by knowledge or slyly converted by creative group experiences. It is rebellious and defensive. Adult educators not aware (ignorant?) of its reigning power in the church either construct meaningless programs or give up on adult education in disenchantment. [Fry 1961, pp. 5–6]

As a strategy to bring about change, education is valued by society because of its respect for the individual's autonomy, but granting this personal liberty greatly lessens its success rate. Education is just one of the aspects of Christian ministry that promote change and growth. It has its limitations; it is impotent whenever individuals determine not to commit themselves to God or the Christian belief system. Human sin can easily thwart the most carefully conceived educational program. (A similar problem plagues the secular sphere. Youth continue to drive recklessly in spite of mandatory driver's-education courses in many states.)

The dark side of human nature prevents us from designing a Christian-education program that will be 100 percent effective. Since true Christian education places the responsibility for learning and change upon the student and not upon the teacher, its outcome can be predicted but not assured. The learner can always choose to go another way despite the prayers and planning of the teacher.

The Importance of Teaching About Sin
Rather than Sins

The Christian life is not a short sprint, but a long marathon journey. Consequently, we cannot survive the assaults and ordeals of this life simply by summoning all our will power to do what is right. To survive the race, to win the race, we have to be motivated from the inside out so that we actually yearn to do what is right. Eagerness to do right is a far better condition, and a more pleasant one, than simply willing oneself to do right. Furthermore, God is not satisfied with mere conformity. He wants us to love him with all our hearts, minds, and strength (Deut. 6:5). God is no more pleased with grudging obedience than a parent is with a child who is outwardly compliant, but inwardly hostile.

Many events and thought patterns contribute to our growth in joyful obedience. One of them is a proper view of sin. When we see the depth, persistence, and hideousness of our sin, there arises the possibility of true transformation. Seeing our sin for what it is need not lead to despair—it can lead to spiritual liberation. When we see the true depth of our sin instead of merely being embarrassed over individual sins, we are prompted to seek the grace which can heal. On the other hand, when we respond to our sin problem by saying, "I'm all right," or "I'm really doing better; it's been a long time since I lost my temper," we are not open to significant transformation. It is our *sin*, not just our *sins*, that must be dealt with. Within us is a contradictory caldron of self-destructive, egocentric, self-protective, sensual, control-seeking lusts that breed the sins we hate. It is right to attack this sin from the outside by ceasing our destructive behaviors, but it is far more important to work from the inside out to reduce the pull sin has on our life (Crabb 1988).

When we see the gravity of our sin, we will then, and only then, be open to receiving God's transforming grace through God-ordained disciplines and ministry. But when we see visible individual sins as our problem, we are content to just muster more self-discipline and go our merry way, attacking sins here and there as if they were isolated weeds in a garden. A teacher who uses clever devices to induce students to enumerate all the sins in their lives will not lead them to see the grip sin has on them.

When we regret our sins of omission (good things left undone) as keenly as our sins of commission (bad things done), we have begun to understand sin. And when we, like Daniel in his great prayer (Dan. 9), acknowledge that we have participated in the sins of our nation and grieve over these wrongs, we have opened one of the windows to true inner transformation. Furthermore, it is often through our dealings with the unlovely that we catch a glimpse of the sin that pulls us into self-centered and hurtful acts.

Christian Maturity

Central to the aim of Christian education is the promotion of Christian maturity. Christian education properly tends to focus on individual Christians, in the hope that as they mature, the church as a whole will mature. Christian education seeks to enable the Christian to glorify God more fully and to participate more deeply in the life and service of the church. In the Bible, Christian maturity is associated with four basic concepts: spiritual autonomy, spiritual wholeness, spiritual stability, and wise use of knowledge.

The first mark of Christian maturity is spiritual autonomy. Spiritually autonomous individuals have control over their lives and are appropriately self-directed. They are in sufficient control of their lives to be able to offer their bodies as living sacrifices that are holy and pleasing to God (Rom. 12:1). To submit to the lordship of Christ requires being in charge of one's life so as to be able to present it to the Lord. Without appropriate self-direction, believers cannot mature in their relationship to Christ. Unfortunately, many churches view autonomy as entirely negative, equating it with self-indulgence. But how can we surrender our lives to Christ if we do not control them?

The second mark of Christian maturity is spiritual wholeness, a quality described in verses like, "Love the LORD your God with all your heart and with all your soul and with all your strength" (Deut. 6:5). Such wholehearted devotion to God is a quality that a person at any age or level of mental or physical development can attain. Moments of complete commitment to God can be seen in children, adolescents, and adults. To be spiritually whole, then, is "to give all that you know of yourself, to all that you know of God." The critical factor in spiritual wholeness is not quantity of knowledge or training but quality of the dedication, giving 100 percent of oneself. An aged Christian saint may possess more knowledge and devotional skills than a child, but both can commit all of themselves to God.

Spiritual wholeness is the central ingredient in Christian maturity. One does not grow roses by gluing petals on rosebushes, and likewise one does not create mature Christians by simply attaching more and more "Christian" behaviors to immature believers. The roots are the most important part, and the root of truly Christian behavior is wholehearted dedication to God. Where this dedication exists, habits of holiness will form that enable a person to live more and more frequently in a state of spiritual wholeness. In the New Testament such people are described as being perfect, complete, or mature.

We should not think it presumptuous to speak of a Christian's being perfect, for both Christ and Paul mention this possibility. Christ's command, "Be perfect, therefore, as your heavenly Father is perfect" (Matt. 5:48), at first glance seems impossible to fulfil. Jesus, however, was neither diminishing the holiness of the Father by suggesting that humans could match it, nor was he giving an offer of salvation none of us can attain. We must note the context of this command. In the previous verses Jesus contrasted the ordinary self-interested love of humans with the self-giving love of God. He spoke of God's ability to love both friend and foe, righteous and unrighteous, and indicated that, just as the Father uses all his resources completely to love, so we must love everyone as best we can within our human limitations. To be perfect or whole means loving as selflessly as we possibly can. Paul summarized his ministry as one that sought to "present every man mature in Christ" (Col. 1:28, RSV). Christian maturity is possible, but not inevitable, for those who open themselves to the working of God's grace in their lives.

In his words to the rich young ruler (Matt. 19:16–22), Jesus spoke of spiritual wholeness: "If you want to be perfect [whole, complete, mature], go sell your possessions and give to the poor" (v. 21). Jesus had diagnosed the young man's malady as loyalty divided between money and God. To become spiritually mature he had to become spiritually whole by repudiating the enslaving claims that money and self had over his life. The young man was being told that only through radical trust in Jesus could he be freed of enslavement to himself.

The third mark of Christian maturity is spiritual stability. This is not the same as psychological stability; the so-called even-keeled individual is not necessarily more mature than the more emotional or moody Christian. Like waves of the sea, spiritually unstable Christians are in a constant state of flux. They have weather-vane theologies that shift and turn with the latest currents of thought. Paul notes that God's spiritual gifts (e.g., pastors and teachers) are intended to bring an end to this situation, to foster maturity: "Then we will no longer be infants, tossed back and forth by the waves, and blown here and there by every wind of teaching and by the cunning and craftiness of men in their deceitful scheming" (Eph. 4:14). Spiritual stability is acquired over time and grows with proper response to the trials and doubts of life. Consequently, it is a characteristic that will be strengthened through one's spiritual pilgrimage. Perhaps only those who have suffered or had sufficient empathy with the trials of others can truly be spiritually stable.

Finally, the idea of Christian maturity is linked with wise use of knowledge. Spiritually mature persons understand the significant issues of the faith and can use this knowledge to inform their lives and teach others. In contrast, the immature can handle nothing but spiritual milk.

"But solid food is for the mature, who by constant use have trained themselves to distinguish good from evil" (Heb. 5:14). Mature Christians understand the essentials of the faith and are able to work with these truths to shape lives. Their knowledge is not used to impress others, but to give glory to God.

Theology is crucial to Christian education. Often Christian education has been accused of drifting far from orthodox theological teaching, particularly in regard to the Christian view of human nature and spiritual growth. This drifting is unfortunate, for Christian education is lost unless grounded in biblically based teaching. No matter how much zeal a Christian educator may have, it is of little use without an awareness of the essential theological underpinning of the faith. When Christian educators understand the importance of growing in relationship with God, the true purpose of the Bible, the role of the Holy Spirit in teaching, the implications of human nature for the learning process, and the essence of spiritual maturity, they will be equipped to lead others in plotting their life maps and growing in grace. Without this understanding, Christian education is reduced to programs and activities that have no higher goal than making church members feel content about the time they spend at church and the money they give to the education budget.

= 4 =

Contemporary Approaches to Education

In this chapter we will present three very different approaches to education. All of them have secular origins and eventually made their way into Christian education. They differ in the teaching methods they advocate and, more importantly, in the control beliefs by which they are shaped. Our task in this chapter will be largely descriptive—to understand these approaches in their own terms and uncover the assumptions that lie behind them (see Kohlberg and Mayer 1972).

Our teaching methods have usually been caught from our own teachers. There is nothing necessarily wrong with such subconscious imitation of other educators, but at the same time Christian teachers should self-consciously examine the way they teach. Many of the habits we pick up restrict the power of the gospel in our lives, and certain teaching strategies can have a similar effect upon our instruction. Christian teachers need to ask themselves, Why do I teach the way I do? Many Christians have unwittingly subscribed to a secular approach to education, having picked it up from their school days. It is difficult to escape from the patterns of one's culture, but Christians must be wary of uncritically adopting the methods and educational values of an alien society. Christian teachers must continually ask themselves whether they are truly being Christian in their educational approach.

Romantic: The Teacher as Gardener

We will use the term *romantic* to describe certain educational tendencies that were present in the classical romantics of the eighteenth and nineteenth centuries. Romanticism had a decisive influence on nineteenth-century thought, in much the same way that modernism has influenced the twentieth century. In this section the romantic's celebration of the imaginative, the childlike, and the expressive is stressed. The romantic approach to education places great emphasis on the metaphor of organic growth and maturation. The physical growth of a plant is the guiding image of the educational romantics. The old saying "Tall oaks from little acorns grow" captures their emphasis on growth. Other orientations also use this metaphor, but the romantics pursue it with a unique vigor and enthusiasm.

Rousseau: A Classic Romantic

In his *Emile,* philosopher Jean Jacques Rousseau (1712–1778) passionately articulates a romantic philosophy of education. Rousseau describes how he educated a boy who was entrusted to his care. This fictional story, which paints a picture of child rearing that has gained many adherents, is filled with educational principles and images drawn from horticulture. Rousseau goes to great lengths to present his approach as the *natural* one. His way—following nature—is marked by freedom and attention to the primordial rhythms of nature in the child. On the opening page he explains that "plants are fashioned by cultivation, men by education" (1962, p. 11). This horticultural image is used to express the aim of the romantic educators: the farmer desires healthy crops; the educator desires mental health and happiness for the individual student. "Romantics hold that what comes from *within the child* is the most important aspect of development; therefore the pedagogical environment should be permissive enough to allow the inner 'good' (abilities and social virtues) to unfold and the inner 'bad' to come under control" (Kohlberg and Mayer 1972, p. 451 [italics added]).

A seedling comes with all it needs to mature into a full-grown plant. All the gardener has to do is carefully nurture it. He certainly does not need to add anything to the plant. His task is not to glue petals on the lilac bush nor to wire fruit on the apple tree. Likewise, children are essentially complete in themselves, and education consists primarily in drawing out their already whole inner resources and knowledge. Education should be concerned more with helping children blossom than with giving them information they do not want or need.

In its extreme forms, educational romanticism is quite deterministic. Nature, it is said, has determined what each person is best equipped to do. Just as petunia seeds produce only petunia plants, and marigold seeds develop only into marigold plants, so certain persons are best suited to unfold into farmers, others into lawyers, and still others into plumbers. The teacher's job is to enable them to do what nature has equipped them to do well. No child is to be forced into another's mold.

The Romantic View of Self

The metaphors of organic growth and nurture reflect the romantics' conception of the self. Romantics view every self as unique and desire that each one be allowed to blossom according to its preprogramed pattern. Just who or what is responsible for the programing is not clear. Romantics generally appeal to Nature—whatever that may mean—as the guiding force. Christian educators who lean toward the romantic approach may view God, however vaguely defined, as the divine programer. In any case, the self has certain needs which are roughly analogous to the physiological needs of animals. The sensitive educator must meet these needs without stifling the child. Rousseau wrote, "The supreme good is not authority, but freedom. The true freeman wants only what he can get, and does only what pleases him. This is my fundamental maxim. Apply it to childhood and all the rules of education follow" (1962, p. 35).

Autonomy and self-actualization were Rousseau's goals. Romantics doubted that any culture or religion possessed anything valuable enough to justify forcing it on the next generation. Reading, the multiplication tables, and Christian doctrine were not deemed important enough to risk crushing the tender young child under their weight, unless the child showed an interest in them (Rousseau assumed that most children would not). If no interest was shown, then the mental health of children might be ruined by forcing on them something that nature had never destined them to desire. Rousseau declared, "When I get rid of all the usual tasks of children in this way I also get rid of the books which are the chief cause of unhappiness to them. Reading is the greatest plague of childhood" (1962, p. 51). This theme was forcefully stated in our own century by G. Stanley Hall:

> The guardians of the young should strive first of all to keep out of nature's way and to prevent harm, and should merit the proud title of defenders of the happiness and rights of children. They should feel profoundly that childhood, as it comes fresh from the hand of God, is not corrupt. . . . Before we let the pedagogue loose upon childhood . . . , we must overcome the fetishism of the alphabet, of the multiplication table, of grammars, of scales, and of bibliolatry, and must reflect that but a few generations ago the ancestors of all of us were illiterate . . . there are many who ought not to be educated, and who would be better in mind, body, and morals if they knew no school. What shall it profit a child to gain the world of knowledge and lose his own health? [1901, pp. 24–25]

For romanticism, the self is of supreme worth, and its development must not be hindered by any claims of society or the church.

Oddly enough, brutality is not unheard of in the permissive classrooms and schools that embrace the romantic view of the self. This brutality is not by the teachers, but by students whose actions go unchecked because the instructors are reluctant to impose their will on a child. In *The Silver Chair,* C. S. Lewis depicts the torment that two students underwent at Experiment House, a thoroughly romantic environment where teachers "cared" so much that they would not punish a child who violated the school's norms.

> These people had the idea that boys and girls should be allowed to do what they liked. And unfortunately what ten or fifteen of the biggest boys and girls liked best was bullying the others. All sorts of things, horrid things, went on which at an ordinary school would have been found out and stopped in half a term; but at this school they weren't. Or even if they were, the people who did them were not expelled or punished. The Head said they were interesting psychological cases and sent for them and talked to them for hours. And if you knew the right sort of things to say to the Head, the main result was that you became rather a favourite than otherwise. [1953, pp. 1–2]

Lewis put his finger on a rather grim aspect of some "free" schools. His observations have been documented by others. In an extensive study of elementary schools in Britain, researchers found that informal or open classrooms proved to be anxiety-producing for many students:

> Pupils whose attributes include a high level of anxiety and neuroticism . . . work harder and are more attentive under formal teaching. These findings suggest that formal teaching contains or controls the overt behavioural manifestations of personality whereas informal teaching allows or

encourages them. This is no doubt because informal teachers wish to foster self-expression in their pupils, but it should be recognised that this seems to lead to more behaviour which tends to work against effective learning—such as general social gossip, gazing into space or out of the window and various negative behaviours. [Bennett 1976, pp. 156–57]

Instead of being liberating, permissive classrooms, with their unclear expectations and their tolerance of unacceptable, even brutal behavior, actually cause many students emotional distress.

Romantic Religious Education

In religious-education circles, educational romanticism has generally appeared as a permissive, experience-centered approach. It frequently claims to be based on scientific data that enable educators to understand how children develop, what they are like in the various stages of maturation, and how best to foster their growth. The term *child-centered* is often used to describe this orientation, meaning that the needs and inclinations of the child, rather than content (i.e., doctrine, biblical subject matter, church history), are given primary consideration when designing an educational program. The needs of the child determine the subject matter; there is nothing so worthy or noble that it can legitimately be forced on a child.

Some writers in the romantic tradition recognize a genuine need for religious instruction. They assert that each person possesses an innate religious outlook which the teacher must help to blossom into a healthy faith. The teacher, however, must not try to make this intrinsic religious impulse conform to any sort of orthodox or traditional understanding. Religious education must foster the growth of a healthy personal faith but show little concern about its particular content or form. In *Changing Aims in*

Religious Education, Edwin Cox argues that religious education should exist to help the child select a religious orientation. The training should not promote a particular orientation to religion, except in cases where the child must be guided away from what is judged to be an unhealthy form of religion. "There is a growing feeling that religious education ought to be, in the jargon of today, 'open-ended.' This means it should have as its aim the giving to children of a religious view of life and then allowing them freely to make up their minds how this view shall express itself both in belief and practice" (1966, p. 66).

This open-ended approach to religious education has achieved considerable influence in the United States since the early part of this century. The Religious Education Association (REA), founded in 1903, and its journal have widely disseminated these views. The membership of the REA was drawn from traditions which supported a highly individualized and humanistic conception of religion (Schmidt 1983, p. 59). The REA maintained that through open and loosely structured instruction the child would best experience God and express his or her religious orientation. The influence of the romantic orientation on the Sunday school has been documented by Robert Lynn and Elliott Wright, who note how the emphasis in the early nineteenth century on the child's need to obey God's law and repent of sin was widely supplanted at the end of the nineteenth century by the theme "Jesus wants me for a sunbeam." "While orthodox churchmen and the 'religious educators' quarreled bitterly in the first decades of the twentieth century, they were united in one crucial respect: both embraced, though in varying degrees, the common ideal of the child as 'sunbeam,' a notion largely foreign to their evangelical ancestors" (1980, p. 84). The child as sunbeam is not entirely a romantic notion, but it does typify the romantic influence on the Sunday school, standing as it does in such stark contrast to earlier views of the nature and need of the child.

The romantic approach has made remarkable inroads into evangelical Christian education at all levels. The self-ism of the 1970s led to widespread acceptance of the romantic ideal of individualistic growth. Some of the clearest examples of this orientation are to be found in various Bible-study guides, marriage-enrichment materials, and the writings of motivational preachers.

Bible-study materials which encourage "personal involvement" at the expense of a careful study of the text often have a romantic orientation. For example, one study of Jesus' parable of the lost sheep (Luke 15:1–7) suggests: "Picture yourself as the lost sheep. How did you get lost? Why were you left behind? How did you feel when the Shepherd came back and searched for you?" (Howard 1973, p. 36). Notice that the students are invited to read any of their present feelings into the passage. There is no attempt to dig into Christ's message in the parable; rather, the passage is to serve as a springboard for personal sharing and self-disclosure. The emphasis here, as in so many Bible-study guides, is on getting the students to talk and share their feelings about the Bible. Growth, it is assumed, will automatically follow.

Discussion is a popular word in Christian-education circles. Many Christian educators believe that any discussion is inevitably educative. They are sadly wrong, for no method in and of itself is necessarily educative. The mere sharing of feelings about Bible passages may strengthen relationships, but it will do little to equip believers to carry out the responsibilities of their priesthood. Bible-study guides which imply that transformation comes through a sharing of feelings rather than through intensive study of the Bible are modern manifestations of the romantic approach.

The romantic approach can be taken in preaching as well as in classroom situations. Sermons which emphasize an individualistic religion and self-fulfilment have strong romantic overtones. Such overtones can be seen in Robert Schuller's *Self-Esteem*, in which he places a strong

TABLE 1 **The Romantic Approach to Education**

Aim	Personal growth and self-fulfilment
Focus	The individual
Educational process	Unfolding inborn traits and characteristics (which are assumed to be good)
Concept of knowledge	Experiences and activities which help a person grow

emphasis on personal growth and maturation. Schuller contends, "There are basically two kinds of persons: those who are individuals and others who are really invalids. I refer to this as 'individualism' and 'invalidism' " (1982, p. 87). The emphasis in the book is upon individualistic self-development and prosperity. Such an emphasis leads to focusing more on filling people's wants and needs than on equipping them for service as believer-priests.

Contributions of the Romantic Approach

In a society where people yearn for affirmation, the romantics are seen as a breath of fresh air because of their stress on personal growth and positive feedback. Romantic educators have reminded all educators of the vital role played by the social and emotional environment of the classroom and have urged that education be more human and less mechanical. These modern disciples of Rousseau have done much to set aside the concept that children are simply little adults. The romantics honor and value childhood and have helped educators to view it not as a time of limited abilities, but as an opportunity for meaningful learning.

The romantics have also taught us to pay attention to the gifts and passions of the teaching staff. Effective leaders know that the staff person who is a round peg in a square hole does not help a ministry team function well. But when the passions and gifts of the individual members are taken into consideration, utilized, and linked, the ministry flows forth with an attractive naturalness and ease. To achieve this goal, we must begin with the assumption that God has spiritually gifted each person in a unique way and that our ministries will be most effective when we operate accordingly. Instead of seeking to shape, control, and add to the resources of the individual staff member, we should begin with the assumption that each of us has something unique to offer and that the discovery of that gift is a remarkable find. The New Testament makes it clear that our ministry should arise from our gifts and passions rather than from a sense of duty alone.

Rousseau's orientation has profoundly influenced both secular and religious education. Romanticism has served as a needed corrective to some of the dehumanizing forms of education that have appeared throughout history. The romantic tradition reminds us that persons are of great value and are more than minds to be filled with knowledge. While the romantics have enriched our practice of education, it would be incorrect to assume that only they are concerned about care and affirmation. Genuine personal respect for students is displayed by advocates of each of the orientations presented in this chapter.

Transmissive: The Teacher as Technician

Transmissionists use a different set of powerful images to express their educational orientation. The factory, with its efficiency, use of science, and output of uniform products of high quality is the guiding image of the transmissive approach. The goal is to transmit efficiently a cultural or religious heritage to the next generation. Consequently, advocates of this approach describe themselves as *content-centered.*

The Factory Image

The student is viewed as raw material to be shaped and modeled into a desired product. As in a factory, cultural transmissionists particularly value efficiency. Behavior modification, adoption of scientific methods, and utilization of educational technology, with its clear behavioral objectives, are all attempts to make the educational process more efficient.

The factory image should not be understood to mean that education needs to be harsh, odious, or machinelike. It is the efficiency and scientific techniques of the factory that attract the transmissionist. Transmissionists are well aware that students often learn best in warm and supportive environments, and therefore they try to make their classrooms cheery places in which to learn. They often are as sensitive as romantics to individual differences among their students. The romantic educator, however, focuses on the individual and celebrates each person's uniqueness, while the transmissionist emphasizes the larger group and seeks to bring the student into conformity with its values.

The factory image also suggests the transmissionist's desire to mold students into a desired shape by conveying to each one the knowledge, beliefs, and dispositions that the larger group values. Mortimer Adler's *Paideia Proposal* develops this theme: "The course of study is nothing but a series of channels or conduits. The child goes in at one end and comes out at the other. The difference between what goes in and what comes out depends upon the quality of learning and of teaching that take place throughout the journey" (1982, p. 49). Even Adler, who is a member of the humanistic wing of the transmissive approach, uses the assembly-line image—raw material in and finished product out—to describe his proposed curriculum. According to the romantic approach, students possess innately all that they need; but in the transmissionist approach they are seen as lacking certain things (i.e., knowledge, habits, skills) which education is to supply.

The Use of Content

The distinguishing mark of the transmissionists is not their concern about content, but the way they use content in education. All the major contemporary theories of education utilize our cultural heritage, as found in books, people, technologies, and societal patterns, but they differ in how they view and use this subject matter. At the risk of oversimplification, romantic educators are pre-eminently concerned about the growth and happiness of the child. They would rather have a happy and well-adjusted illiterate than a well-educated but stifled conformist. Transmissionists, on the other hand, see themselves as more realistic; after all, they reason, people have to hold a job and contribute to society. Transmissionists are willing to sacrifice the momentary happiness of the individual for the greater good of the society, nation, or Christian community. Most transmissionists believe that an individual who conforms to the larger group and acquires valued knowledge or skills will be happier in the long run than the person who, in the passion of a moment, decides that he or she does not need to learn to read or do math or speak in public. The focus on basic life-skills in many state-mandated curricula reflects the view that learning socially valuable techniques is more important than childhood happiness. While both transmissionists and romantics may care deeply about students, the romantic places highest value upon personal freedom and choice, and the transmissionist values those things that will help the student get ahead and enjoy the good life.

The Hard and Soft Faces
of the Transmissive Approach

The transmissive approach to education is split into two orientations which share the same basic goals but differ widely in their programs. In the *technological* orientation the factory image is taken to its logical conclusion. Education is viewed as a process that can be analyzed and controlled like the manufacture of dishwashers, cars, or computer chips. Schools fail because they do not apply science to education in the same ways and to the same degree that industry uses science to increase productivity.

The *humanistic* (in the best sense of that word) orientation is less mechanistic. It likewise values efficiency, but it does not see education as primarily a scientific enterprise. Education is an art, and in teaching students the instructor must take into account the passions, interests, and humanness of the students.

These contrasting forms of transmissive education can be seen in two actual approaches to the teaching of literature. In the technological approach the materials are organized in what is judged to be the most efficient manner. Students read portions of great texts of literature that have been scientifically selected. The teachers believe that it is unnecessary for students to read an entire book if they can deduce its general ideas from a much smaller selection. The students work individually and occasionally consult the teacher, who primarily serves as a resource person and record keeper. They study each portion until they are able to pass an objective test. Then they move on to the next selection.

In the humanistic approach the students study books and long selections that the teacher believes represent high points in literature. The teacher frequently reminds the students of the great value of literature and urges them to make the books and authors they are studying their lifelong friends and companions. In short, the instructor seeks to inspire them to read, learn, and love great literature. Instead of emphasizing objective facts the teacher through Socratic questioning draws from the students interpretations which he or she approves.

These two approaches demonstrate certain similarities:

Someone other than the students chooses the materials to be studied.

There is a stress on getting the right answers (although the processes used to fix the right answers in the student's mind are vastly different).

Mastering rather than using the material is stressed.

Learning the subject matter is thought to be inevitably humanizing or growth-producing.

Yet there are also certain basic differences:

The humanistic approach is more concerned about the student's developing a positive attitude toward the subject matter.

The humanistic approach exploits the dynamics of class interaction to motivate and inspire. Since classroom interaction is subjective, the technological approach downplays it.

The technological approach values efficiency over appreciation, teamwork, or the satisfaction of reading a whole book.

The technological approach places greater emphasis on testing. It is thought that mastery of a selection can be scientifically measured through objective questions.

Both the hard and soft faces of the transmissive approach to education are flourishing today. In Christian-education settings the soft face is more often seen, but some Sunday-school workbooks and curricula reflect the technological approach. It is in Christian day-schools that the technological orientation has had its greatest impact. The Accelerated Christian Education (ACE) program represents the technological wing of the transmissive approach taken to its logical extreme. After completing a two-week training program, a pastor is ready to set up an ACE school. No teachers need to be recruited, and none of the usual school equipment is necessary. With a monitor in place, the school is ready to run.

ACE directs its newly minted school principals, or "supervisors," to set up individual carrels or "offices," where [the students] study silently with their workbooks for three or four hours daily, letting a cartoon character named ACE and his friends teach them everything from elementary reading to high school history and "creation science."

The room is neat and quiet: When students need to go to the bathroom or sharpen a pencil, they raise a religious flag to get the attention of the supervisor. If they have a question concerning their work, they signal with the American flag. [Barringer and Vobejda 1985]

The children use flags so as not to "waste time holding their hands up." A more person-oriented transmissive approach to Christian education would look vastly different but would share the same basic thrust of passing on valued knowledge and skills to a relatively passive student (passive not in the sense of being inactive, but in the sense of being shaped from the outside and viewed as a receptacle into which the educational process deposits material for later use).

Religious Forms of Transmissive Education

The content which the teacher transfers to the students varies widely among religious groups. Liberals who seek to instill an open and thoroughly modern outlook in their students can be as transmissive as fundamentalists who desire that their students subscribe to a detailed doctrinal statement and memorize numerous Bible verses. Transmission does not refer to the rigidity of the subject matter nor to the precise method of instruction. Transmissionists use lectures, discussions, and Socratic questioning, to name just a few of their methods. The essence of the transmissive approach is its aim of internalizing the values, knowledge, and beliefs esteemed by the teacher. In contrast, the romantic approach seeks to allow the child to unfold into his or her destined form.

Christian-education programs which emphasize traditional schooling and place a high value on the retention

TABLE 2   **The Transmissive Approach to Education**

Aim	Efficient transmission of valued knowledge and skills
Focus	Society, the nation, or the church
Educational process	Mental absorption of factual information
Concept of knowledge	Highly organized factual information

of factual information are following a transmissive approach. Selected passages from the Bible seem to support this approach, but taken as a whole, the Bible advocates education which goes beyond the transmission of religious information or the shaping of behavior. The Bible calls us to have educational programs that are liberating and that provide persons with a deep, unshakable sense of meaning. Christian education should actually empower persons to live responsibly before the Lord.

In some extreme forms, transmissive education fosters an unhealthy dependence on teachers. The students know that the teacher will give them the answers, and so they become more and more passive, expecting to be spoon-fed. Christian education must not support an educational consumerism in which students, being unable or unwilling to satisfy their own basic spiritual needs and those of others, simply consume the spiritual truths imparted by a teacher. Christians are not just to partake of spiritual nourishment; they are to use it to strengthen their ministry.

Contributions of the Transmissive Approach

Many educators follow a transmissive approach, and with good reason. In Western societies, where education is universal, the transmissive stress on efficient use of educational resources makes sense. Transmissionists seek to maximize the educational gain from each dollar and hour invested, and few persons in a world of limited resources and great needs can oppose that desire. The transmissionists' interest in knowledge, right answers, and covering the material often translates into an effective no-nonsense approach to teaching and learning. Another positive contribution is their willingness to curtail rampant individualism, because transmissionists believe that there are higher values than the individual's likes and dislikes.

This approach seeks to distribute valued knowledge and skills as efficiently as possible. The focus is not on the individual, as it is with the romantics, but on the larger group. Unlike Rousseau, cultural transmissionists will try to teach an unwilling child to read. They argue that our society is a better place to live when people are literate. The good of the nation, society, or the church is considered to be more important than the good of the individual.

Developmental: The Teacher as Coordinator

John Dewey and Developmentalism

As an educational philosophy the developmental approach dates to the late nineteenth century and the work of John Dewey (1859–1952). In essence, Dewey applied to education the tenets of several of the then fashionable schools of thought—pragmatism, thoroughgoing empiricism, and Darwinian evolutionism. Dewey himself was an open antagonist of supernaturalism. While he considered himself to be religious, his understanding of religion and divinity was vastly different from an orthodox understanding of the Christian faith. He dabbled in religion and religious education throughout his life and in the end developed his own peculiar and thoroughly "scientific" faith. His educational philosophy, however, is only incidentally connected to his religious views.

Dewey began his academic career at a time when philosophy and psychology were considered to be partners in exploring the nature of humankind. In some universities the experimental-psychology faculty were listed as members of the philosophy department. Thus, it should not be a surprise that at the heart of Dewey's philosophy of education is his view of psychology.

Dewey separated himself from both the romantics and the transmissionists. He was not the first person to advocate the basic principles of developmental education.

Such principles can be found in ancient Greek texts and throughout the history of educational philosophy. He was the first, however, to articulate a comprehensive developmental philosophy of education. In brief, he sought to promote development of the child primarily through the child's interaction with society and the environment.

The Essence of Developmentalism

The romantic educator conceives of knowledge as consisting of meaningful experiences which help peel away the layers of the self until the person's inner core shines through. An apt analogy is the peeling away of the skin of an onion. The transmissionist views knowledge as boxes of factual information which can be stored in the warehouse of the mind. If these boxes are arranged in a neat and orderly manner, the knowledge deposited in them becomes even more valuable. Consequently, transmissionists evaluate educational programs primarily on the basis of their efficiency in disseminating highly organized knowledge. By contrast, the developmentalist sees knowledge as a *tool* which helps the person make sense out of the world. Christian knowledge is to serve as a map for the believer on his or her pilgrimage. It provides a perspective on life that helps us understand our trials, joys, and sorrows.

Developmentalists seek to promote an *instrumental* use of knowledge; that is, they want the student to be able to do something with the knowledge that has been learned. The romantic asks if the child has had a meaningful experience reading the Bible. The transmissionist wonders if the child rightly understands the passage. The developmentalist inquires whether the child can use his or her knowledge of the passage.

The Child as Scientist

The guiding metaphor for Dewey is the child as scientist. The child is neither a flower which simply needs to unfold nor raw material which needs to be molded, but rather a scientist who is seeking to make sense out of the world. Dewey contended that all persons are scientists in that they spend their lives in forming hypotheses to solve problems. They come up with more-adequate ways of solving problems not simply through learning more hard facts, but through developing better ways of processing their observations. Life confronts people with very difficult situations—the death of a loved one, intense personal pain, and vexing ethical questions such as what constitutes a proper response to the issue of riches and poverty—and people develop "theories" to deal with the problems inherent in these situations. According to Dewey, humans are always working to understand their complex world more fully. In seeking to answer the questions of life, we develop explanations that help bring order to a highly confusing situation.

Our personal building of theories or explanations of the world has a parallel in the way science forms its theories. A famous example of a paradigm change in scientific thinking is the switch from a Ptolemaic to a Copernican view of the universe (Kuhn 1970, pp. 68–70). The Ptolemaic view, which regarded the earth as the center of the universe, was developed in the second century before Christ and served admirably for many centuries. It did not work well at certain points, however, and had to be refined and modified until it became excessively complex and unwieldy. The Copernican theory, which posited the sun as the center of the universe, was far simpler and incorporated new astronomical data far more easily than did the Ptolemaic theory.

The theories or mental maps that we carry around in our heads about what the world is like shape the way we live. One person's theory of the causes and purpose of suffering leads to bitterness, resentment, and self-pity, while another person's view, even in the midst of suffering, leads to patience and a love for the essentials of life.

I recall a Sunday-school teacher who wisely exhorted our class to consult the Bible about life's problems, because it is the "Owner's Manual for Life," written by the "Manufacturer." He was right. If our mental maps accurately reflect reality, we will find life more satisfying and our service more effective. A thoroughly accurate mental map can be obtained only by careful study of the Bible.

Developmentalism and Relativism

Some Christians have been hesitant to embrace a developmental approach to teaching and learning because they view it as inherently relativistic. To them, developmentalists see everything as evolving and changing. There seems to be no stable ground in such a system, no sure place to stand. Undoubtedly some developmentalists hold such views, but relativism is certainly not a necessary feature of developmentalism. In fact, the major twentieth-century secular proponents of developmentalism have not been thoroughgoing relativists, and most, although not accepting Christian values, certainly have not embraced a values-neutral approach to teaching and learning.

Historically, relativistic educators have most frequently adopted the romantic or transmissive approach. It should be no great surprise to find relativists numbered among the romantics. Relativistic education thrives on the individualism and selfism found in the romantic approach. (Believing that no value or norm is valid unless individuals choose it for themselves, and knowing that individuals are bound to make different choices, relativists deny that any particular set of values is universal.) Similarly, transmissive educational programs, especially moral-education programs in public school, often have a relativistic base. Many transmissive education programs fall into the trap of teaching values established through sociological analysis; in other words, they simply pass on the values of the majority. The teachers' task is to train students to accept and practice the values held by the dominant culture. Often these educators appear to be far from relativists because they are quite outspoken in their support for a particular set of values. But the basis of their holding a given value may not be an absolute ethic but simply the present cultural climate. I can still recall some well-intended sex-education films I saw in junior high that were based on an ethic no deeper than "we do this" and "we don't do that." Since such presentations lack an ethical base, they can do no more than endorse current behavior. They hold to a weather-vane system of ethics which shifts its position with every wind of cultural change.

But there is nothing inherently relativistic about developmentalism, though it puts great stress on the notion that all of us approach life from our own perspective. All of our observations and perceptions of the world around us are filtered through a mental grid. Developmentalists, then, insist that there is no such thing as an unmediated perception of reality—a perception that is the same for all persons regardless of their background and development. But to say that each person has his or her own lens for viewing reality is not in itself a relativistic assertion. Even the Mosaic law recognized that human perceptions differ. That is why it required testimony from two or three witnesses to convict a person of a capital offense (Deut. 17:6). Presumably the need for several witnesses reflects concern that even the most well-intentioned witness may have misinterpreted what happened. Paul also understood that perceptions differ; he asserted, for example, that the natural man simply cannot grasp certain things about the spiritual world that are immensely meaningful to the spiritual man (1 Cor. 2:14–16). Both may observe the same phenomenon or read the same text, but they will assign completely different meanings to what they have observed or read. The difference is not in what is perceived, but in the way meaning is assigned.

Christian developmentalists have an absolute metaphysic but a relative epistemology. They believe that there are unchanging and reliable absolutes in the universe (absolute metaphysic), and yet at the same time they acknowledge that one's perceptions of God and the world are conditioned by one's own mental structures and experiences (relative epistemology). The developmentalist is not a skeptic but recognizes the conditional nature of all our perceptions.

Because developmentalists place such an emphasis on the conditional nature of our knowledge, it may seem that they regard truth as relative. If this were true of developmentalism, the Christian would be well advised to reject developmentalism as an educational theory for the church. But is it not true that our *perception* of the "faith that was once for all entrusted" (Jude 3) is not identical with the faith actually entrusted to us by God? Too often evangelicals have given the same status to theology that they rightly give to the Bible. The Bible is nothing less than the Word of God, but theology is a human product, an interpretation of how we understand this once-for-all faith. Theology is culturally conditioned and affected by the theologian's mental grid and human finiteness.

Figure 3 shows that theology stands in the same relationship to the Bible (special revelation) as science does to creation (natural revelation). Both the Bible and creation are the products of God's work, but our interpretations of them bear the shortcomings of any human endeavor. To argue that theology can be refined is no more an indictment of the Bible or God's changeless character than the fact that geologists contradict one another is a charge against the goodness of God's creation. Theology and science are human interpretations of God-supplied data. We must never suppose that our interpretations are so authoritative and certain as the objects of our study.

The developmentalist seeks to help Christians gain a more useful knowledge of the faith and to encourage them to work out an understanding of their beliefs that fits the world as they see it. The Christian developmentalist ac-

Figure 3   Revelation and Human Inquiry

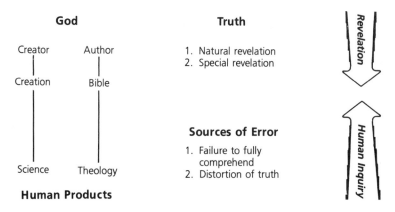

Based on a diagram by Rodney McKean.

cepts Scripture as bedrock and is guided by the major councils of the church and the rich heritage of theological writings, but also recognizes that each age and ultimately each person must answer the question of what it means to be a Christian.

Experimental Support

Jean Piaget (1896–1980) provides empirical evidence for Dewey's more speculative thinking. While Dewey advocated the scientific method, he left it to others to validate his theories empirically. Piaget found that children do not passively absorb knowledge—rather, they construct it. Two classic experiments of Piaget are of interest here. In one, young children were shown two identical beakers of water. Upon questioning by the experimenter, the children agreed that both beakers contained the same volume of liquid. However, when the water from one beaker was poured into a third beaker of greater diameter, with the result that the water level was lowered, the children claimed that the third beaker contained less water. They did not realize that the dimensions of the beaker did not affect the volume of water. Children learn concepts like volume only by having their initial hypotheses (e.g., "water level is the measure of its volume") disproven through various experiences. From sharing drinks with friends to helping a parent measure liquids, children discover that their original ideas are faulty. Only rarely is such hypothesis testing done verbally, and verbal instruction alone (e.g., "Children, the volume of a liquid is not affected by the dimensions of its container") does little to help generate a more adequate hypothesis. The important point here is that children do not (in fact, cannot) absorb the relationship between volume and dimensions from a single experience or through verbal explanation. Our minds are constantly at work developing and refining hypotheses (i.e., subconscious explanations or mental patterns) which help us make sense of the variety of experiences we have every day.

The second important experiment by Piaget, which concerns the constructive aspect of memory, was reported in *Memory and Intelligence* (1973). It is one of numerous studies demonstrating that our memories are not simply deep freezes from which material comes out in the same form in which it was put in. Small children were shown a row of ten sticks which regularly increased in length from one end of the row to the other. A week later they were asked to draw a picture of how the sticks looked. The drawings tended to depict the sticks as the children would themselves have arranged them. For example, some children who did not as yet grasp the concept of a graded series recalled seeing two groups of sticks, "big ones and little ones." These results suggest that memory is not so much a photographic image as a reconstruction reflecting our own peculiar mental patterns.

Another fascinating result of this study was obtained when the children were retested eight months later. They were asked to draw a picture of the sticks they had seen

eight months earlier. Those children who had advanced in
terms of their mental operations produced more-accurate
pictures than did those who had not advanced. A child
who eight months before had drawn only a few sticks in
graded order might now draw most of them in the right
order. The accuracy of the drawings increased with the
development of more-advanced mental hypotheses. Again,
the memories were not so much photographic images as
reconstructions according to one's personal mental patterns. In his description of this experiment Piaget noted
that the evolution in the accuracy of the children's drawings "did not take the form of a sudden leap from incorrect
to correct drawings, but was in the nature of a very gradual
progress from one stage or sub-stage to the next, as if the
memory were linked to the development of the preopera-
tional schema" (1973, p. 41).

Every person is constantly striving to understand the
world, to generate mental patterns and habits which allow
one to operate with efficiency in a complex environment.
Piaget believed that we humans automatically seek to find
a mental balance with our external circumstances. This
process can be enhanced by educational programs which
are rich in experience, interaction, and reflection.

Use of Content

John Dewey in *Experience and Education* decried the
tendency in education to follow one of two extremes. Educators tended either to focus entirely on the subject matter (cultural transmissionists) or to ignore the formal
content altogether (romantics). Dewey lamented, "On the
one hand, there will be reactionaries that claim that the
main, if not the sole, business of education is transmission
of the cultural heritage. On the other hand, there will be
those who hold that we should ignore the past and deal
only with the present and the future" (1938, p. 78). Developmentalists do not reject textbooks and disciplined
study. They simply use these means in different ways and

for different purposes than do cultural transmissionists. The developmentalists' unique use of content will become clear as we explore some of the basic ways in which the transmissive approach differs from developmentalism.

First, cultural transmissionists view the student as being essentially passive and in need of external motivation. The student's mind is viewed as a blank slate to be written on or, alternatively, as a lump of clay ready to be molded. The student is in essence a complex recording device, like a tape recorder or camera, well equipped to take in and preserve information which is presented.

When the student is viewed as essentially passive, methods are often favored which are thought to transmit verbal information most efficiently. The teaching process is seen as a pipeline or conduit of information, and, following the factory image, its success is measured primarily in terms of quantity and efficiency. Developmentalists do not downplay efficiency, but they realize that it is only one of many criteria of success. If efficiency were the only criterion used to judge the culinary arts, then microwave ovens would be universally employed. However, taste, texture, appearance, and aroma are judged to be more important in cooking than is efficiency. Likewise in education the quality of the learning and the student's reaction to the educational process must be considered. Quality learning is difficult to measure empirically and, like good food, is best judged by a connoisseur who truly understands it.

A further result of viewing students as essentially passive is that they are considered to be so lazy that they will not willingly undertake learning. Consequently, it is necessary for the teacher to motivate the child through rewards and punishments. An unwelcome corollary of this practice is the notion that the more distasteful a learning experience is, the more educative it must be. Little is done in such circumstances to cultivate a love for learning or self-discipline. Developmentalists, on the other hand, seek to encourage students to become self-starters and eager learners who are not dependent on external rewards.

Second, the cultural transmissionist has a unique view of the subject matter: knowledge of the subject matter is viewed almost as an end in itself. The material being taught is often thought to possess a transforming power. A knowledge of the "Great Books," for example, is believed to inevitably produce high-mindedness. Christians with this orientation conclude that what the "Great Books" can do, the Bible can do even better. They then proceed to fill their students with factual information about the Bible. Developmentalists do not disparage the accumulation of factual information from and about the Bible, but they see such information as a means to an end. They agree with the old quip that the Bible was given not for our information but for our transformation.

Third, the world of the cultural transmissionists is essentially static. They believe that the big issues of life remain the same from generation to generation. Like perennial weeds the same problems and issues keep popping up from year to year. Thus a person who has learned the right answers to today's basic questions is prepared to answer whatever crucial questions may arise in the future.

Developmentalists view the universe as dynamic and complex. New issues and questions arise which call for more than just application of the knowledge and skills of the past. Change is increasingly a hallmark of our world. Alfred North Whitehead noted that until the first quarter of the twentieth century, the time span of a major cultural change was usually longer than a person's life, and thus it was appropriate to view transmitting culture as the primary task of education; but now education must be seen as continual inquiry (Knowles 1973, pp. 159–60). Certainly a basic set of religious and ethical questions exists, but they must be addressed in unique cultural, political, and historical settings. The answers to yesterday's questions will help us answer the questions of tomorrow, but they are not themselves the answers to those questions. Learners need to be equipped to think and act Christianly in circumstances and environments which will be vastly different from the ones in which they receive their education.

Cultural transmissionists and developmentalists are both concerned about teaching content. However, they use the content for very different purposes. Dewey saw the task of education as equipping students to synthesize and balance the ambiguous data of human observation in sophisticated ways. He did not disparage the cultural heritage but hoped that education would produce students capable of going beyond the current understanding of this heritage. George Forman and David Kuschner, contemporary educators who share Dewey's concern, have written *The Child's Construction of Knowledge,* in which they show that emphasis on the child's construction of knowledge does not mean that we ignore our heritage.

> Self-regulated construction of knowledge does not mean that the child must reinvent the wheel and begin where early man began. It does mean that the child mentally constructs the basic relation between structure and function (round-means-roll), even though the wisdom of his culture places him in situations that make that invention highly probable. . . . Intelligent behavior results from an interaction between the natural operations of the mind and the accumulated knowledge of the culture. [1977, p. 6]

A religious educator who takes a developmental approach is as concerned with *how* students think about their faith as with *what* they think. The developmentalist is concerned that they gradually acquire a more sophisticated and accurate way of handling the complexities of the faith. Such an educator holds that if in considering, for example, divine sovereignty and human responsibility, individuals simply shut their eyes to one truth or the other, they have not developed the mental operations essential to a mature faith. The developmentalist emphasizes the ability to balance and integrate the complex and ambiguous data of the Bible, personal experience, and observation of the natural world. Christian education should work to facilitate the development of a lifestyle of reflective Christian thought and action. Individuals so equipped will walk confidently in a complex and changing world because their values are not just hand-me-downs from the teacher but are values they personally own. Their values have developed from reflection on their tradition (e.g., the Bible and their church's theological orientation), their experience with God (e.g., in regeneration and prayer), their current practices, and the values and practices of other believers.

Contributions of the Developmental Approach

The romantic educator focuses attention on enabling the inner person to blossom, and the transmissionist concentrates on conveying external facts. The developmental emphasis on interaction helps integrate these two conflicting views of the aim of education. Also, the developmental emphasis on the instrumental use of knowledge and the importance of bringing the structures of thinking to maturity have helped educators move beyond mere transmission of information or behavior modification.[1]

A Christian Response

Now that we have examined these three approaches to education, one might rightly ask, "Which one is the most Christian?" Such a question needs to be asked because we must seek vehicles for teaching the gospel which nei-

1. There are many fine teachers who do not think of themselves as developmentalists but who actually teach in a developmental fashion. What really counts is not what they claim to do, but what they actually do in the classroom. Thus their advocacy of a particular educational orientation may be of little significance. However, educational leaders in the church need to be able to articulate a clear philosophy so that they can shape the instructional methods of the teachers for whom they are responsible.

TABLE 3   **The Developmental Approach to Education**

Aim	Equipping the learner with useful mental tools
Focus	The individual in society, the nation, or the church
Educational process	Building a map for life through interaction between present experiences, personal perspective, and the accumulated knowledge of society, the nation, or church
Concept of knowledge	A tool to be used

ther deform it nor rob it of its power. However, the question proves impossible to answer for at least two reasons. First, all three approaches allow for a great deal of latitude and variation. It is possible to find examples of each approach that are unacceptable models for Christian education; by contrast there are other examples that would harmonize well with the gospel. For instance, a romantic-oriented seminar on spiritual gifts might focus on one of two basic emphases: (1) Exercising spiritual gifts is a way we find fulfilment. When we do what fulfils us, we are using our spiritual gifts. (2) God has given each of us spiritual gifts. Through service and the counsel of others, we can discover those gifts. We best serve when our ministry fully utilizes our specific gifts and passions. While this second emphasis has a strong romantic orientation to it, it is also quite compatible with the biblical concept of ministry. However, the first emphasis is far too self-oriented to qualify as a fully biblical understanding of spiritual gifts.

The second reason for difficulty in determining which of the three approaches is most Christian is that they can be used in two very different ways. They can be used as the underlying philosophy for a narrowly focused, self-contained ministry in the church or for the entire Christian-education program. It is appropriate for a Bible study that has the explicit purpose of serving as a support group to adopt the romantic approach, that is, to focus on sharing and personal needs. It is quite another matter for a church to adopt a thoroughgoing romantic approach for all of its activities. We must bear in mind that many situations will be best served by a mixture of educational approaches. While a church may have an overarching orientation that is best described as developmental, some of its specific ministries may be decidedly romantic or transmissive in nature. Which approach works best or is most Christian will depend in large measure on individual circumstances.

5

Transformational Christian Education: The Teacher as Guide

In the preceding chapter we discussed three major approaches to education. Examples of each one can be found in contemporary Christian-education programs. Unfortunately, none of them provides for our educational task a comprehensive blueprint which is theologically accurate and results in the deep inner change that true religion should foster. The romantics fail to give adequate attention to the fall. Theirs is a sunny world in which children naturally choose what is best for themselves, but need to be protected from the societal pressures that could warp them. In the romantic approach the teacher helps the students to unfold, to strip away the obstacles to self-actualization which have been imposed upon them by society, and, if they so desire, to ponder their God in a self-chosen fashion. This individualistic orientation, with its ethic of "if it feels good and doesn't hurt others, do it," runs counter to the biblical witness. The romantic approach knows very little about the costs of discipleship and almost by definition is plagued by purposelessness. The romantics fail to realize that meaning is not found in self-oriented searches for it, but comes as a by-product of service centered on God and others. The romantic focus on the students' needs and self-discovery often degenerates into a hedonistic approach in which the immediate desires of the students determine what takes place in the class session.

The transmissionists too often merely pass on knowledge without affecting lives. Religious educators with this orientation frequently make the well-intentioned mistake of confusing knowing God with knowing about God. Transmissionists tend to have immediate goals, but often teach without an ultimate purpose. These teachers typically think in terms of covering so much material or having students memorize this verse or scrutinize that map. Quite often the short-term goals become ends in themselves with the result that all the activity and learning simply lead to more activity and learning.

The developmentalists, following the radical humanist John Dewey, frequently downplay the value of our religious heritage. This approach places such an emphasis on the learner's reflecting on his or her experience and constructing a more adequate personal theology that the Bible and historically important doctrines are often given a secondary place. Developmentalists can become so obsessed with the conditional nature of our perceptions that they become very skeptical about the absolutes of faith. Also, the developmentalists appear far too optimistic about our ability to understand and learn from our experiences. The field of psychotherapy points to the difficulty of perceiving and interpreting our experiences in ways that lead toward growth. Many people require years of intense personal coaching and guidance to understand their patterns of relationships and values. "Learning by doing," the maxim of the developmentalist, provides all educators with a good reminder. However, not all doing leads to learning. Practice will certainly make permanent, but not necessarily perfect.

The crucial job of equipping believers to carry out the responsibilities of their priesthood cannot be accomplished simply through Christianizing one of the secular theories of education we have discussed. An alternative approach is needed that embodies the educational principles implicit in Jesus' ministry and in the faith-nurturing practices of the people of God in both the Old and New Testaments. One such alternative approach to Christian education can be called the transformational approach, because it seeks to foster a radical change in learner-disciples by remaking them from the inside out through the working of God's grace. By contrast, romantics assume the inside is fine as it is and seek to peel away the layers of the outside that hide the true inner self. Transmissionists believe that persons are changed from the outside in. Only developmentalists place a similar emphasis on change from within, but they tend to see it as a relatively simple process of adjusting one's perspective and acquiring new categories of thought.

The Goal of Transformational Christian Education: Discovering God-centered Meaning

Unlike the other approaches to education, which have secular and religious roots, the transformational approach is decidedly spiritual at its very core. The transformational approach builds most directly on the human search for God-centered meaning. Our birth is not an accident of time and chance, but God has a purpose for each of us. In the words of the Westminster Catechism, we were created "to glorify God and to enjoy him forever." And within each person there is a deep sense that life should have meaning. While many choose to worship idols instead of the living and true God, those idols are a testimony to the human soul's quest for meaning. Thus the aphorism that the two greatest days in a person's life are the day of birth and the day one finds out why one was born is really true.

The transformational approach begins with the assumption that there is a purpose for our lives. However, this purpose is not found in a self-oriented search for meaning, but as a by-product of a life given in service to others and guided by a renewed mind and values. We must underscore that personal meaning is discovered by the learners; it can never be handed to them by a teacher. Nor can it begin to guide and shape a life until the individual involved has seen it validated in his or her own experiences. Once our personal meaning has been validated in this way, we can have the integrated life Viktor Frankl described when he echoed the words of Friedrich Nietzsche, "Those who have a *why* to live can bear with almost any *how*" (1963, p. 121).

The transformational educator operates with an eye toward enabling persons to discover their God-centered meaning. However, when the pursuit of meaning becomes the end of Christian education, it will not be found. Therefore, transformational education has before it three long-term goals which produce a climate in which life-directing meaning can be found: (1) the equipping of believer-priests for service and worship; (2) the cultivation of a servant's heart and skills; and (3) the establishment of a teaching environment that is open to the working of God's renewing grace.

The Content
of Transformational Christian Education

If changing people from the inside out is to be reality and not merely a wish, educators must come to their task knowing what they must teach, how it should be taught, and who should teach it. The content used by the transformationalist is rich and varied. The transformationalist educator affirms the rule of Scripture over the entire educational process and seeks to construct a Bible-oriented program which is open to personal experience, rich in worship, and reflective of his or her own devotional life. Such a program will comprise several major elements:

1. *Guidance as to how best to follow Jesus.* A Christian disciple is one who makes doing what Jesus did the first priority in life and formulates plans to realize this goal (Willard 1988). When we talk about what Jesus did, we need to be careful not to focus our attention on the high moments of his life. New believers will be frustrated if they set out to copy what Jesus did during his public ministry. The forgiveness he extended to his enemies while he was on the cross did not come through clenched teeth and by sheer will power, but out of genuine pity and desire that they not suffer for their dreadful act. We offer Christians little practical assistance when we urge them to imitate the public ministry of Jesus without letting them see what his source of strength was. Christians cannot hope to emulate the single-mindedness and spiritual power of Jesus simply by trying to copy what he did in public.

The way we begin to follow Jesus is to do what the private Jesus did: he prayed, he fasted, he spent time in solitude, he lived in submission to God, he sought out the unlovely, and he meditated. We will live as Christ did when he was in public view to the degree that we live as Christ did in his private moments. At the heart of transformational Christian education is this practical and concrete instruction for people of all age levels.

2. *Knowledge of Scripture and its practical application.* Biblical literacy, a topic discussed further in chapter 8, is central to a program of Christian education. A knowledge of the Scriptures will be most useful in a context where learners are encouraged to live out the principles presented. This does not mean that every lesson must have an explicit application. In fact, some application-oriented lessons actually work against learners' doing the Word. The applications in some lessons are so specific and so

narrow in scope that people are able to fulfil them without ever having their basic values or commitments challenged. Doing the Word of God, however, involves far more than simply making some minute changes.

3. *Knowledge of God and appropriate worship.* The church at worship and at prayer is a powerful means of personal transformation and a striking witness to the world. How do we establish and cultivate worship in the church? We can achieve this goal in part by teaching people about the God who is worshiped. But we must also teach people *how* to worship. We must resist so objectifying Christian knowledge that our students learn about God rather than come to know God personally. Transformational Christian education cultivates the habit of seeking after and enjoying God. Worship and learning are complementary paths to transformation; both must be present in our classes.

4. *Critical reflection on life.* To establish the lordship of Christ, we must examine every area of life in terms of God's priorities. The circumstances and demands of each life are so different that we cannot merely hand people a detailed blueprint, spelling out every value and response for the Christian. Each Christian must construct a personal blueprint for living based on the Scriptures and formed in dialogue with brothers and sisters in Christ. This process of blueprint making will be successful only if we develop the habit of measuring the various parts of our lives by the standard of the gospel.

The Characteristics of Transformational Christian Education

Transformational Christian education is not tied to one teaching method such as discussion, projects, case studies, simulations, or lectures. Whatever method is used, transformational education is marked by clear and effective teaching which opens students to the working of God's grace. Such teaching is characterized by several key features:

1. *A focus on remembering.* One of the chief goals of Hebrew education was to make sure the people would never forget and would therefore always fear God and do his commandments. In Hebrew thought, the chief spiritual malady was forgetfulness. So education had as one of its chief ends remembrance of the mighty acts that God had performed in behalf of his people. We are indeed forgetful pilgrims, and we need to be reminded of the good things that God has done in our lives, in the lives of our brothers and sisters in Christ, and in salvation history. Accordingly, in our teaching we must take time for testimony, reflection, and remembrance. We remember best when concrete examples of what God has done are brought to mind.

2. *God-centeredness.* The religious instruction described in the Bible was remarkably God-centered. And yet not God-centered in the way we might first imagine. It was not God-cenetered in the sense that it focused on theology; rather, the focus was on God himself. Significantly, in several Old Testament occurrences of a common Hebrew word for "teach" and "learn" (*lāmad*), it is the Lord himself who is the Teacher. God taught his people through his interactions with them in day-to-day living. Furthermore, the great and powerful teachers of the Bible, like Isaiah and Jesus, always had a message directly related to the life of their learners, but even more important, it was a God-centered message. Transformationalists constantly show people that righteous and joyful living is available only to those who look at life through God rather than, as is the usual case, at God through life.

3. *An emphasis on relationships.* Christian education is most healthy when it takes place in a context marked by strong and vibrant relationships. These relationships provide the background and support for transformation

to occur. Healthy relationships can furnish a sense of belonging, models to emulate, encouragement, esprit de corps, and positive expectations. Many educators have observed the power of a strong relational context to foster openness and encourage change. However, the more "scientific" and efficiency-minded educators tend to dismiss the relational focus as unnecessary or even counter-productive. They are sadly wrong: their emphasis on efficiency has blinded them to an invisible but truly essential aspect of Christian education.

In our society, justice is usually thought of as fair play or equal treatment; but in the Bible, justice or righteousness is thought of as fulfilment of one's relational responsibility. The just or righteous person is one who carries out the responsibilities of his or her relationships. Since fulfilment of relational responsibility is a mark of righteousness, we must model and teach integrity, respect, and commitment in relationships. E. R. Achtemeier comments that in the Bible each relationship "brings with it specific demands, the fulfillment of which constitutes righteousness. The demands may differ from relationship to relationship. . . . When God or man fulfills the conditions imposed upon him by a relationship, he is, in Old Testament terms, righteous" (1962, p. 80).

An appropriate emphasis on relationships is essential to transformational Christian education not only because good relationships enhance learning, but also because our relationships define our responsibilities. The issue is broader than learning to like the people in our church or Bible-study group. Remember Christ's teaching in the parable of the good Samaritan: our relationships extend further than we often like to admit.

4. *A sense of mystery and wonder.* The true transformationalist operates on the assumption that how we learn is as important as what we learn, and that Christian education must be conducted with a sense of mystery, wonder, awe, reverence, and beauty. We are far better at lis-

tening to stories than we are at processing information. We make more sense out of our world through metaphors than through bare hard facts. This truth is reflected in the emphasis which Christ's teaching method placed on story, and in the fact that story is used in the Bible more frequently than any other literary genre. Christ could have conveyed theological truth in the form of abstract dogmas. Instead, he told stories about ordinary people and about how their lives reflect aspects of the kingdom of God.

Christian education must take advantage of the aesthetic dimension of humankind, the dimension that is marked by stories, song, music, drama, imagination, and beauty. This does not mean that education should take the path of least resistance and use only methods that are highly pleasing. Discipleship means hard work! And yet, discipleship training does not have to be a drudgery.

5. *A balance between support and challenge.* Christian education is concerned with changing people. People change most readily when they are in environments that foster change. Such environments are marked by both support and challenge. Learners will open themselves to change when they sense that they are in an environment where change is encouraged (i.e., where challenges are issued) and where they feel that they are affirmed and that setbacks are not fatal (i.e., where there is support). In environments marked entirely by challenge students generally do not take risks because the costs of failing seem too high. By contrast, teaching situations that are marked entirely by support often do little more than preserve the status quo; the students are not encouraged to make the significant changes that will lead to true, liberating transformation.

At the heart of transformational Christian education is the working of God's grace. The teacher needs to open the student to God's transforming power. The class atmo-

TABLE 4   **The Transformational Approach to Education**

Aim	Transforming the learner
Focus	The individual in the body of Christ as a potential recipient of God's grace
Educational process	Interaction between personal experiences and transforming truths, as one opens oneself to the working of God's grace
Concept of knowledge	A tool to be used as God intended

sphere must be permeated by a reverence for God and a respect for persons. The teacher must seek, through moments of worship, prayer, an openness to God's work, instruction, exhortation, and care, to be an instrument that brings God's power to bear on the lives and problems of the people in the class.

Tragically, far too much Christian education today is plagued by purposelessness. Mere activity is not enough to tackle the problems Christian education is called to address. The transformational approach can provide a sense of purpose and direction that will enable one to have a "ministry of meaning." Educators who take this approach view the process of promoting spiritual growth and maturity as both a divine and a human affair. They believe that ultimately only God's renewing grace can bring spiritual transformation, but that God's grace is made available only to those who have been trained to open themselves to it through disciplined and righteous living.

A transformational approach to Christian education is not tied to any one method or instructional strategy. It demands, however, that the teacher be more than a mere technician. The teacher must experience a growing relationship with God and have discovered, by doing what Jesus did, what it means to live as Jesus lived; otherwise the teacher will fail to expose the students to the working of God's grace.

= 6 =

Social Science and Christian Education

We have considered the aimlessness of what often passes for Christian education today. We suggested that a proper aim for Christian education is to supply biblically based "maps" so that the Christian can find meaning in a confused world. We examined both the biblical basis for this aim and the theological content that must undergird Christian education. In chapters 4 and 5 we looked at four approaches to education and their respective ability (or lack of it) to fulfil our stated aim. In this chapter we will consider the integration of the social sciences and Christian education.

Throughout this century Christian education has been admonished to ground itself in the social sciences. Tremendous benefits were to result from the application of social-science research to the problems and issues of Christian education. However, after nearly eighty years of such admonitions, both the suppliers and consumers of such scientific data are frustrated. The social scientists are frustrated because their work is often ignored or misused,

---

This chapter is an adaptation of Jim Wilhoit, "The Impact of the Social Sciences on Religious Education," *Religious Education* 79 (1984): 367–75. Used by permission.

and Christian educators are dissatisfied because they are not supplied with answers to the questions which they judge to be significant. Despite all the emphasis which has been placed on the role of the social sciences in Christian education, they have only minimal influence on the theory and practice of Christian education today. Educational ideologies, theology, and common sense shape and inform Christian education far more than do rigorous empirical findings. Nevertheless, many leading Christian-education theorists continue to claim that the social sciences can provide the discipline with the clear aim and sense of purpose that theology has failed to deliver. If Christian education is to provide maps for people who are searching for meaning, we do need data on contemporary life and the effectiveness of various educational practices. The social sciences can provide such data.

Obstacles to Integrating Social Science and Christian Education

From George Albert Coe (1917) to Randolph Crump Miller (1956) to James Michael Lee (1973), various writers have lauded and praised the social sciences as a valuable source of information for religious education. Coe and Miller, however, gave us religious education without social science, simply asserting in passing that the latter is valuable. For example, Miller stated that the modern Christian educator "must be competent in educational psychology, developmental psychology, the sociology of learning, and many other scientific disciplines" (1956, p. 39). But despite his expressed concern that Christian education be scientific and empirical, his own writings contain only vague allusions to "psychology and educational research." In their major works on religious education, Coe and Miller do not cite or utilize specific research studies. Coe, a true giant in religious education, was frequently guilty of bolstering his own opinions and limited observations with undocumented appeals to supposedly established principles of scientific education. Lee, on the other hand, has given us social science without religious education. The focus of his writing has primarily been the critique of religious-education theories that are not scientifically based and the identification of social-science data relevant to religious education. He has provided us with a useful summary of behavioristic research but not with a comprehensive theory of religious education.

There are a number of reasons why social-science data have been neither authoritative for nor notably helpful to Christian education, several of which we will briefly examine. It should be noted that they are not fatal objections to the use of the social sciences in Christian education, but they do illustrate the problems involved in such an enterprise. (See Lindblom and Cohen [1979] for a thorough discussion of the problematic role of social-science research in problem solving generally.)

The High Cost of Research

Social-science research is so costly "that it cannot be used for most social problems nor pushed to conclusive answers on those issues on which it is used" (Lindblom and Cohen 1979, p. 40). The problem is compounded for Christian education because federal funds, and even private grants, are difficult, if not impossible, to obtain for projects involving empirical study of religious phenomena. Of course, this problem is not a fatal argument against using the social sciences. It simply stands as a reminder that, in a world of limited resources, only a fraction of the significant questions which confront us can be investigated through formal scientific resources.

Suspicion and Hostility

Valid research findings are often rejected out of hand due to prejudice against the use of scientific inquiry in religious areas. A significant suspicion exists that empirical measurement of faith, spirituality, and Christian maturity is impossible. No matter how robust and valid the findings, the empirical researcher of religious phenomena can expect some rejections simply on the grounds that the research attempted to measure the immeasurable. This certainly is not an indictment of the research methods per se, but it does illustrate how the influence of the social sciences in religious matters is limited by the widespread suspicion that religion is not part of the domain of any science.

The Necessity and Difficulty of Objective Validation

Unique and atypical findings which are the result of a single study are seldom sufficient to change established practices and theories. It is necessary to replicate and confirm the findings before their authority or utility will be recognized. This is especially true if the findings run counter to our orienting paradigms. It may take decades to establish a single principle in a particular area of education.

What has just been said about the necessity of replication may leave the impression that our analyses of research findings are always objective and unprejudiced by our educational ideology, instructional theory, or theology. However, research is never evaluated from a position of evenhanded neutrality. Our prejudices, fears, and presuppositions always play a part in our review of research. In point of fact, if research seems to support what people already believe about the world, they are more likely to view the empirical findings as being valid than if the findings contradict their world-view.

The basic reaction to Lawrence Kohlberg's work on moral development illustrates this point. He set forth a theory of cognitive development that concentrates on the making of moral decisions rather than on behavior. He asserted that a person's moral thinking develops through a process marked by several clearly defined stages. The stages themselves and their order are highly value-laden and reflect Kohlberg's liberal Western individualistic orientation. The empirical basis of his theory was a study done for his doctoral dissertation with about seventy-five boys and a few interviews conducted in various parts of the world (Kohlberg 1968). His study, like any investigation, was flawed at points, and the results were less than convincing (Kurtines and Greif 1974). However, Kohlberg's study received widespread acceptance because it told many people what they already believed. Since it fit so nicely with their ethical theories and educational philosophies, its weaknesses—the small size and homogeneity of the sample—were seldom raised as objections.

We must remember that we never can evaluate and use the findings of social-science research in a completely neutral and objective manner. We will always challenge the research methods and design of those studies whose results seem to us morally obnoxious, but we will look with sympathy on studies of equal quality whose findings we believe to be right (i.e., agree with our position). Social-science research should, however, have an impact on the field of Christian education whenever it produces numerous high-quality studies which clearly support a particular educational strategy. At present, unfortunately, social-science research receives most attention when it simply confirms current practices, beliefs, or prejudices.

The "Is-Ought Problem"

Empirical research is fundamentally incapable of addressing normative issues; it can describe what a situation is actually like but cannot tell what it ought to be. The line between *is* and *ought* may sometimes be thin, yet it is an incontrovertible fact that empirical research by itself simply cannot answer the basic questions about aims, the nature of persons, or the ethical implications of various instructional methods. It is both futile and inappropriate to attempt to derive a normative statement solely from a descriptive statement. Another nuance of the is-ought problem is that science cannot even tell us what problems should be studied, for our values influence the problems we select for scientific scrutiny. Joseph Wood Krutch has said that "though many have tried, no one has ever explained away the decisive fact that science, which can do so much, cannot decide what it ought to do" (1954, p. 31).

Ambiguous and Diverse Findings

One popular picture of the social sciences is that the experimental findings tend to converge and are basically harmonious. Consequently, Christian educators often speak freely about *the* findings of psychology or the social sciences. This view evokes the image of a mighty river fed by diverse sources and flowing ever forward in one great channel. However, a closer examination reveals that experimental results are more like the mythical nine-headed serpent Hydra. When one of its heads was cut off, two appeared in its place. Likewise, social-science research typically leads to more questions and research, not to definitive answers.

There is great divergence in research findings, and thus the value of social-science research cannot lie in its supposedly unequivocal testimony to the nature of persons or of the learning process. Yet there is a tendency toward an idolatry of science. Many persons seeking for norms and truth in a confused world assume that a monolithic and almost godlike science will provide a definitive picture of the world. But science does not provide a foundation of noncontrovertible principles from which one can deduce a theory of Christian education. Indeed, an examination of educational research is usually more bewildering than enlightening. As Arthur Holmes reminds us, the social sciences do not speak with a single voice: "The dicta we often hear, 'psychology teaches . . .' or 'philosophy says . . . ,' are really meaningless. It is individual psychologists who teach, not psychology *per se;* it is individual philosophers who say things, not philosophy itself. Psychologists do not agree among themselves and neither do philosophers" (1977, p. 29).

The problem of divergent findings is compounded when one begins to consider the issue of generalization. Just how far can one extrapolate from a given research conclusion? Do the findings for third-graders hold true for adults? To what degree can missionary educators expect principles which are valid in their homeland to hold true in a different culture?

Due to a variety of factors, social-science research cannot speak with the authority and clarity one might desire. Its cost, the suspicion it arouses, the difficulty of objective validation, its inability to speak on normative issues, and the diversity of results mean that by itself social science cannot provide the foundation for Christian education. Even so, as we shall see, it does have a crucial role to play in our theorizing about Christian education.

Recommendations for the Integration of the Social Sciences and Christian Education

We will now look briefly at six suggestions to help us integrate social science and Christian education. Admittedly, these suggestions primarily focus on correcting certain practices in Christian education that have tended to hinder integration, but they do provide a foundation for a methodology of integrative theorizing.

Abandon the Proof-Text Approach to the Social Sciences

Many Christian educators have taken a proof-text approach to the social sciences. In the current state of affairs it is very easy for them simply to raid the social sciences to support their preconceived educational theories. (It is regrettable that we often use biblical texts in the same way.) We abuse the social sciences rather than use them when we turn to them simply to support a pet theory.

Biblical scholars distinguish between *eisegesis* (reading a meaning into the text) and *exegesis* (drawing out the actual meaning of the text). When we make use of the social sciences, we should be like the biblical scholars and ask ourselves, Are we eisegeting or exegeting? Are we using carefully selected findings to confirm our presuppositions, or are we trying to hear the message of the social sciences in their own terms?

To safeguard against proof-texting, a practice which seems to come quite naturally, the Christian educator should be cautious about making sweeping generalizations such as, "Psychology tells us that . . . ," or "Educational research has established that. . . ." There is no clear unity in the findings of the social sciences; only a proof-texter will pretend to have found it. This practice of making excessively broad generalizations can be significantly curtailed if precise documentation is required whenever reference is made to the findings of social science. Further, we must keep in mind that the social sciences are not the proverbial nose of wax which can be twisted into any shape. Our theories must be held with a degree of tentativeness so that we can hear the possibly dissonant findings of various research studies. Only when we are humble enough to allow our theories to be challenged will the sciences be able to illumine our work.

Formulate Verifiable Theories

To be scientific, a theory must be stated in such a way that it can be tested by empirical examination (e.g., "pure water boils at 100° C"). The fact that the advocates of a particular Christian-education theory can cite a plethora of research studies does not mean it is scientific. A theory is scientific only if it is open to verification by empirical research. By this criterion only a very small amount of current Christian-education theorizing is scientific, for very few of our contemporary ideas are formulated in a way which allows them to be verified through scientific investigation. Christian educators have been hesitant to state their theories in concrete terms. Accordingly, whether they have been successful in meeting their noble but nebulously phrased goals cannot be measured in a rigorously empirical manner.

To say that a theory cannot be verified by empirical methods is not to declare it worthless. (While the basic claims of Christianity are consistent with our observation of the world, they cannot be proven through scientific methods either.) Nonverifiable theories can be of great value, though their usefulness will be different from that of theories which can be subjected to empirical examination:

> An unfalsifiable theory, which is metaphysical rather than scientific, may act as a powerful heuristic in directing pre-scientific conceptual speculation that later can be applied in a more scientific manner. So the Greeks propounded many metaphysical theories, such as atomism and heliocentrism, which helped keep alive ways of asking questions that turned out later to be of enormous scientific significance. [Boden 1979, p. 103]

The lack of interest in stating theories in empirically verifiable terms apparently has two causes: (1) a high percentage of the issues in Christian-education theories (e.g., the need to be reconciled to God) are metaphysical in nature and not open to verification through empirical findings to the degree that hypotheses in other areas are; and (2) the field of Christian education has not encouraged its theorists to subject their ideas to empirical tests. It is hoped that these theorists will begin to have the courage to state the empirically based portions of their ideas in scientifically verifiable terms.

Study the Primary Sources

Early in the study of any discipline, one learns that an examination of the primary sources is mandatory. In a field like Christian education, which seems to be touched by all areas of life and human inquiry, it is easy to allow the pressure of the moment to keep one away from the primary sources. However, real integration is not likely to occur when our thinking is based entirely on secondary and tertiary sources.

The preoccupation of many Christian educators with Piaget's stages of human development probably results from an overdependence on secondary sources. To be sure, the stages are an important part of Piaget's thought, but he is far more concerned with issues of epistemology and the construction of knowledge. In a sense, his stages are little more than the icing on the cake. When the stages are divorced from his theory on the construction of knowledge, they become essentially just another collection of age-group characteristics. It is nothing short of tragic when Piaget's theory of genetic epistemology and interactive developmentalism is turned into a simplistic statement of what children are like at various ages. Digging into Piaget's books may at first be a bewildering experience, but it will disabuse us of the notion that his contribution to educational theory is nothing but a summation of the stages of childhood.

(I was once asked to prepare some training materials which would discuss the "major findings of educational psychology." Considering that to be too broad a topic, I asked for some specification and was told to cover the big principles such as "we can't learn anything meaningful from a lecture—meaningful learning occurs only through discussion." This generalization was seriously suggested as a topic for me to write about, but in fact educational research supports no such conclusion. Obviously the person who made the suggestion had done no reading in the primary sources. She had simply concluded from her personal dislike of lectures that they must be useless.)

Acknowledge Presuppositions

Christian education is inextricably bound to the teacher's values and beliefs. One's educational aim and the content are largely determined by a value complex and set of religious beliefs which the sciences can inform only to a limited extent. We might use the analogy of an outline. Christian educators, because they base their values on the Bible, come to their task with the major points in place and use the sciences as a source of guidance in determining the minor points. The eighty-year history of our discipline demonstrates that one's theory of religious education will primarily be a product of one's values and beliefs and only secondarily a product of scientific data. It is one's implicit philosophy and theology which set the overall agenda for one's educational theory.

The crucial role played by our presuppositions can be seen in an analytical model developed by William Frankena. In his *Philosophy of Education* he graphically represents the interrelationships among the major questions in education (see figure 4). Frankena indicates that a complete theory of education will address five basic questions. Since these questions require answers from different sources (some are questions of philosophy and theology, while others are questions which require empirical data), Frankena's system can provide a helpful tool for clarifying the respective roles of presuppositions and various academic disciplines in our theorizing about Christian education.

Question A concerns one's world-view, that is, one's conclusions about the ultimate purpose of the world and of humankind. These basic issues are addressed academically through philosophy and theology. Such ultimate questions about what *ought* to be simply cannot be answered by the findings of science alone, which deal with what *is*.

Question B calls for a description of the world. The empirical evidence of the social sciences can play a role here, for this question is concerned with how persons learn, how they interact with one another, and what processes promote their development. However, much of the

FIGURE 4   **The Major Questions in Education**

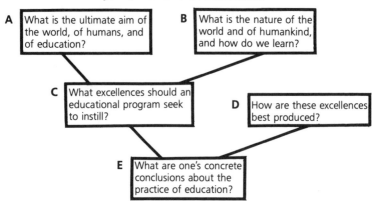

Adapted from William Frankena, *Philosophy of Education* (New York: Macmillan, 1965), pp. 7 – 9.

evidence used in thinking about the nature of the world will come from everyday observations of the world (e.g., what seems to keep children's attention when one is telling a story, or what conditions help people open up in a group). The social sciences simply cannot address all the major empirical questions about the nature of the world. Because of the cost of research, the rapidity of social change compared with the relative slowness of social research, and the complexity of the world, much of our information about the world is necessarily based on evidence drawn from sources other than empirical research. The Christian view is based, of course, on the Scriptures and the traditional teachings of the church.

While the social sciences can supply some data about the nature of people (question B), it would be presumptuous to claim that science can definitively answer questions which have separated religious and philosophical traditions for centuries. It would seem more appropriate for Christian educators to acknowledge their theological presuppositions (such as we have done in chapter 3), the major points of their outline of Christian-education theory, and then to use findings from the social sciences, compatible with their educational approach, to fill in the details of the outline. If this activity is marked by a healthy degree of reflection and intentionality, it can escape being mere scientific eisegesis.

The central question for Christian education in this schema is question C, which is concerned with identifying the excellences which an educational enterprise is seeking to instill or develop. As Frankena states, "Education is the transmission or acquisition of excellences (desirable abilities, habits, states, traits, etc.) by the use of techniques like instruction, training, studying, practice, guidance, discipline, etc." (1965, p. 5). The question is broad enough to allow for the romantic's aim (excellence) of fostering "growth and self-awareness" and for the transmissionist's aim of fostering "traits which promote cultural survival."

The answers to question C are established by synthesizing the answers to the questions about ultimate ends (A) and the nature of the world (B). Question D then asks about the most appropriate methods for producing these excellences. The answer can in part be determined through empirical evidences of the type the social sciences are in a good position to provide. However, due to the paucity of conclusive findings in educational research, most of the data for question D must come from casual observation. For instance, social-science research has been unable to come up with a clear-cut definition of what makes for "good teaching." Yet most educators have put into practice many of the characteristics of good teaching, having drawn them from common sense and random observations. Finally, the answers to both questions C and D are synthesized to produce answers to question E, which is concerned with concrete conclusions about the practice of education (i.e., the curriculum).

Recognize the Unity of Truth

The idea of the essential unity of truth must permeate the integrative process. This concept has been summarized in theological language as "all truth is God's truth." In other words, truth is truth no matter where or how it is found. Unless one is willing to assert that equally valid findings can be uncovered through a variety of avenues of exploration, efforts at integration will prove to be fruitless. A denial of the unity of truth has plagued integrative efforts in Christian education. Individuals who are theologically oriented have tended to deny the validity of scientific findings, and those who favor empirical research have depreciated the validity of data resulting from theological inquiry. A belief in the unity of truth does not lead to the claim that all truth is equally useful in solving a given problem. As was indicated earlier, one's world-view and value orientation will prove to be more relevant in addressing certain foundational issues, but this does not diminish the validity of social-science data. On the other hand, empirical research will be more useful than theology in predicting the immediate effects of various instructional strategies, but that does not negate the value of theological inquiry in Christian education.

Put Science into Action

The biggest impediment to the use of science in Christian education is the prevalent notion that science is more a product (i.e., a body of conclusively established data) than a method of inquiry. The integration of science and Christian education requires educators not just to use the products of science, but to be scientists, in the sense of carefully observing the context and effects of their ministry. Too often decisions regarding one's ministry are based on quick and biased observations that fail to grasp the essence of the situation.

In a world of limited resources and in a discipline seemingly touched by all areas of life and human inquiry, it is not possible for all the data we employ to be based on rigorous empirical research. The science which will prove to be most useful to the Christian educator is the science-in-action of the classroom rather than the science of the laboratory. This is a restatement of the position advocated by John Dewey at the founding of the Religious Education Association. Science understood as a process of controlled and reflective observation should play a significant role in the theory and practice of Christian education. The science which can help our discipline is not a science which sees itself as a treasure chest of uncontested facts about the world, but a science which gives us a way of investigating what the world is really like. In training future Christian educators, an important focus should be on equipping them to be thoughtful, observant, and reflective persons who can do research as they minister.

Our model for the integration of the social sciences and Christian education is not one where the sciences serve as the foundation (an impossibility) nor one where the sciences act as the uncontested experts on certain topics (an inappropriate role). Our model of integration is one of dialogue and interaction among the various legitimate areas which play a part in fashioning Christian education. The best integration will come when we realize that many of the empirical questions of Christian education can be answered only by casual observation. Integration will occur as we test our observations against our theology, our ethics, and our science, lest our observations simply perpetuate our prejudices.

The social sciences do not provide a great data-bank of answers to all educational questions. They are most valuable when we use them to keep us from the sin of egocentrism. The sciences can provide us with data on contemporary issues, data that can be extremely valuable as we seek to guide people in a confusing world. And they can provide data on educational practices, data that may challenge us to re-examine our approaches to education. Christian educators should use such data to challenge and refine their theories, but should at the same time abandon the notion that the data themselves provide a comprehensive and neutral voice in the theorizing about Christian education.

7

Some Findings of Social-Science Research

In chapter 6 we suggested that, while social-science research must be examined and accepted with much caution, there is a place in Christian education for contributions from the social sciences. Many of these contributions are in no way incongruent with the Bible or traditional Christian doctrine. Indeed, if we accept the notion that all truth is God's truth, we will have no trouble accepting (with discretion) the work of social scientists even as we continue to cling to the unshakable truths of Scripture. The findings of the social sciences can provide a valuable perspective on the teaching-learning process.

Most of us look at teaching through memories of our own educational experiences. Our perspective on teaching is usually very personal and experiential, being made up of our recollections of what we enjoyed, benefited from, feared, or hated in our own education. Yet while the most useful and practical knowledge about teaching often comes from our own experience, another perspective can be valuable. In fact, many teachers yearn for a way of seeing teaching, and their own teaching in particular, from a perspective more objective than their own.

Good social-science research, properly used, can provide a teacher with another perspective on teaching and learning. With another viewpoint available, it is easier to break away from the educational maxim, "Teach as you were taught." Educational research does not provide infallible principles or universally useful rules, but if we are willing to look, it gives us a glimpse into the classroom through another pair of eyes. We would all be skeptical of a physician who used no other instrument but a stethoscope. A good physician takes advantage of the different perspectives provided by various tests and instruments. Likewise, educational research can give us information from an angle we might never have considered. In this chapter we will explore several findings that can provide Christian educators with an enriched perspective on teaching.

Meaningfulness and Learning

Meaningful material is learned more quickly and retained longer than material the learner judges to be meaningless. We can see the validity of this principle in our everyday life. On a test three weeks hence, we would find it easier to recall the year of our birth (a four-digit number) than the year the Peace of Westphalia was signed (1648, another four-digit number). Likewise, most of us would find it easier to remember "God is love" than "Ho theos agapē estin" (the original Greek). In a very real and powerful way, meaningfulness affects learning, understanding, and recall.

Educators must realize that meaningfulness is ultimately the decision of the learner. The term *meaningful* is used to describe texts, lessons, and experiences that are judged by the student to be significantly life-related. Each student decides whether or not a subject is meaningful. From an educational perspective there is no content, not even the Bible, that all learners will judge to be meaningful. Since meaningfulness is dependent upon the judgment of the individual student, we are simply not able to select materials that all will judge to be significantly life-related. In other words, we can lead children to Sunday school, but we cannot make them learn. Teachers must do all they can to make a subject attractive, but they should never take upon themselves the students' responsibility for learning.

Educators must also recognize that *meaningful learning* is not necessarily the same thing as *learning meaningful material.* The latter involves learning some sort of content that has objective value—the Bible, for example. It is possible, however, to learn meaningful material in a rote, or meaningless, way. A motivated person could memorize a book of the New Testament and in the process never come to understand the book or its implications for life. A big mistake of some well-intentioned lay teachers is to confuse learning meaningful material with meaningful learning. All too often they enter the classroom expecting that, because the lesson derives from a book of objective worth, the class will experience meaningful learning. The bored looks of the students, however, should quickly tell the teacher that meaningfulness is not guaranteed by the source of the lesson. Again it is clear that it is each student, not the teacher, who ultimately decides whether a subject is meaningful.

If a student judges material to be life-related, understanding and remembering will follow. Meaningful learning is marked by three features: (1) the students both understand the individual parts of the lesson and see the big picture; (2) they perceive the significance and importance of the material; and (3) they relate the new material to their previous knowledge. The research evidence clearly supports the maxim that what we judge to be most meaningful we also understand and remember best. David Ausubel (1969) and others have conducted numerous studies demonstrating that a focus on meaningful material results in faster learning, better retention, and vastly superior integration with previous knowledge. The troublesome gap between life and the classroom is significantly narrowed by meaningful learning. (Figure 5 shows that meaningful material is retained much better than is material learned by rote. Of course, churches do not have final exams, but they do have rough equivalents. For example, children may be offered external rewards—stars, candy, or trips to camp—if they master their lessons by a certain date.)

In addition, meaningful learning is readily transferred to life. Application of learning is a real concern in any type of education, but looms particularly large in Christian education because of its desire to affect the way students actually live. This is not an automatic process, but research studies show that it is certainly fostered by an appropriate emphasis on meaningful learning. Well-under-

FIGURE 5   **The Retention of Meaningful and Rote Learning**

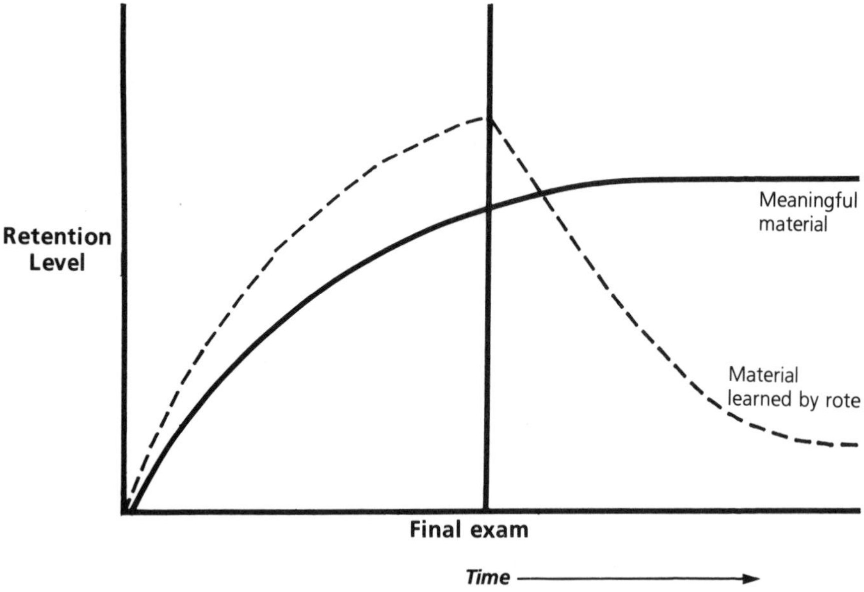

Adapted from Stanford C. Ericksen, *The Essence of Good Teaching* (San Francisco: Jossey-Bass, 1984), p. 7.

stood concepts have far more power to shape our lives than do facts that are only hazily perceived.

Various studies illustrate that meaningful instruction can be readily transferred to new situations. In a classic case (Brownell and Moser 1949; Cronbach 1963, p. 342) children were taught subtraction involving two-digit numbers and borrowing (e.g., 95–29). Among the variables was that some children experienced meaningful learning, others experienced mechanical learning. Half of the students learned to borrow and subtract by learning mechanical rules. They learned to perform the steps necessary for solving the problems but did not understand the general concept of borrowing. The other half were shown why borrowing is necessary and were thoroughly taught the concept. At the end of the instructional period, the students were tested on their subtraction skills. The scores were similar, those in the group that received meaningful instruction doing slightly better. A real difference showed up, however, when the students had to transfer their learning to a new situation. In a subtraction test involving three-digit numbers and borrowing, the students in the group receiving meaningful instruction did significantly better than those who had learned the rule mechanically. Meaningful learning paid off in the long run because it could be generalized. On the basis of this study and similar ones, Lee Cronbach concluded:

> Here is strong evidence for choosing teaching materials that can be understood, and for teaching by methods that produce insight. In choosing between equally correct procedures or explanations, one that can be more fully and deeply understood at that time is to be preferred. Sometimes it takes additional effort to put the meaning across, and teachers are tempted to take a short cut by teaching a prescription. But in teaching a body of subject matter quick and easy gains are less important than returns over a long period. [1963, p. 344]

In promoting meaningful learning, we need not fall victim to a consumer-oriented Christian-education program. Our emphasis on meaningfulness should be read not as a new plea for educational romanticism, but as a simple reminder that students will learn what *they think* is important to them. Teachers, though, can affect what their students view as important. Here are four suggestions:

First, convey a sense of personal interest in and excitement about the material. One of the fastest ways to deaden a lesson is to apologize to the students for "having to cover this material; I know you won't find it interesting [because I don't], but I am supposed to go over it." Showing excitement can be hard for introverted teachers, but a full effort must be made to show that the lesson material is personally vital, related to life, and engaging. Students tend to project the positive feelings they have for their class and teacher onto the subject being studied. In a class marked by a warm atmosphere and a teacher who is respected, students will have more positive feelings for a subject than in a class whose atmosphere is judged to be less than congenial. Education does not take place in a vacuum. The teacher has the powerful tools of class atmosphere and personal warmth to affect the quality of learning.

Second, know the material backward and forward. To teach something in a meaningful way, the instructor must know it well enough to think on his or her feet and adapt to class changes, questions, and misunderstandings. If a teacher does not have a firm grasp of both the details and the big picture, it is virtually impossible to foster meaningful learning. In such cases the teacher will generally talk in vague generalities or lose students in a desert of dry facts.

Third, do not try to cover too much material. All of us can benefit from following Alfred North Whitehead's "two educational commandments, 'Do not teach too many subjects' and again, 'What you teach, teach thoroughly' "

(1929, p. 2). When teachers try to cover too much material in too little time, by necessity they place a higher value on covering the material than they do on the student's understanding it well.

Fourth, give more attention to principles and patterns in the material than to its specific details. We use the expression "to know it by heart" to describe rote memorization; a better phrase would be "to know it by head." To know something truly by heart, one would so deeply understand it that it could provide guidance, comfort, and challenge in one's life. If Christian education is to reflect the fact that Christianity is meaningful, it must constantly stress principles and their applications.

The Influence of Student Attitudes

The meaningfulness of material and one's ability to remember it are directly related to one's system of beliefs. Learners are less likely to remember material that goes against their values or belief system. Two studies that dealt with learning controversial facts demonstrate the connection between attitude and learning. In one of them (Levine and Murphy 1943), two small groups of equally bright college students, one pro-Communist and the other anti-Communist, carefully read two persuasive texts, one anti-Communist and one pro-Communist. After reading the texts the students were tested for recall of the materials once a week for five weeks. The results of the study are quite striking. The anti-Communist students not only learned anti-Communist materials more quickly than they did pro-Communist materials, but they retained them better as well. Likewise, the pro-Communist students fared better with the pro-Communist materials. For example, in the final test the anti-Communist students scored an average of 52 percent on the anti-Communist section, whereas the pro-Communist students averaged only 16 percent. Similarly, the pro-Communist students scored much higher on the pro-Communist section. In both initial learning and in recall, the learners' attitudes provided a good predictor of performance.

An earlier study by Allen Edwards (1941) yielded similar results, though not as clear-cut. College students were tested on their learning and recall of texts explaining the New Deal. Here again a relationship was found between a person's political persuasion and retention of material. Material that supports one's values is more quickly learned and better retained than material that conflicts with them.

The findings of these classic but now dated studies continue to be supported by current research, although investigators do differ in their explanations as to exactly how attitudes affect learning. A recent massive review of research studies on students' attitudes toward science and the effect upon their achievement in science is instructive at this point. The reviewers found that attitude is correlated with achievement in science, though it is not as important as cognitive ability. What is most pertinent here, however, is the finding that attitude and achievement feed on one another: "Comparison of the various ability, achievement, and attitude correlations suggested that one is perhaps most likely to feel positively toward science as one actualizes one's ability through science achievement" (Steinkamp and Maehr 1983, p. 389). In other words, success in a given area tends to foster positive attitudes toward the subject matter, which in turn make achievement in that area more likely. There is nothing like the power of success to help students overcome a negative attitude toward a subject. Nor, when it comes to strengthening one's commitment to the faith, is there anything like seeing a biblical truth work in one's own life.

Students clearly are not simply passive receptacles of information. Their attitudes, beliefs, and life goals affect how and what they learn. Fostering a positive attitude toward the material being studied is not optional; it is necessary if quality learning is to take place. The schoolteacher's quip about a student's having "an attitude problem" is often an accurate diagnosis of the hindrance to learning.

Folk wisdom regarding Sunday-school teaching says, "It doesn't matter if the students understand. Just have them learn the lesson; it will help someday." Of course, we all remember and use knowledge that we learned in educational settings that we disliked. But social-science research indicates that learning will come naturally and the quality of the learning will be much greater if the students care about the subject and think it is valuable.

The Importance of Big Ideas

Education designed to foster meaningful learning places a premium on the big ideas of the subject that is being taught. Learning will never be meaningful if students perceive that they are being bombarded with just a stream of facts. Whitehead thought that a preoccupation with isolated facts has a deadening effect on education: "Education with inert ideas [i.e., isolated facts] is not only useless: it is above all things, harmful. . . . It must never be forgotten that education is not a process of packing articles in a trunk" (1929, pp. 1–2, 33). The fundamental concepts of a subject should be stressed since they provide the learner with a means of efficiently organizing the material so that it can be mastered more easily.

The subjects in a notable experiment were asked to recall the following passage after reading it once:

> The procedure is actually quite simple. First you arrange items into different groups. Of course one pile may be sufficient depending on how much there is to do. If you have to go somewhere else due to lack of facilities that is the next step; otherwise, you are pretty well set. It is important not to overdo things. That is, it is better to do too few things at once than too many. In the short run this may

not seem important but complications can easily arise. A mistake can be expensive as well. At first, the whole procedure will seem complicated. Soon, however, it will become just another facet of life. It is difficult to foresee any end to the necessity for this task in the immediate future, but then, one can never tell. After the procedure is completed one arranges the materials into different groups again. Then they can be put into their appropriate places. Eventually they will be used once more and the whole cycle will then have to be repeated. However, that is part of life. [Bransford 1979, pp. 134–35]

One group of subjects read through this paragraph without having been told its topic. When asked to recall what they had read, they had an average comprehension rating of 2.29 out of a possible 7.00. Another group was told, prior to reading the paragraph, that the topic was "washing clothes." Their comprehension rating was 4.50. Obviously, a grasp of the basic concept can greatly enhance learning.

First, a grasp of basic concepts proves to be a great aid to memory. Concepts provide hooks on which to hang individual facts. Without a framework to which the details and subtleties of a lesson can be attached, they will slip through the cracks and be lost in a distressingly short time. Jerome Bruner comments, "Perhaps the most basic thing that can be said about human memory, after a century of intensive research, is that unless detail is placed into a structured pattern, it is rapidly forgotten" (1960, p. 24). The rate of decay for unattached facts is indeed very quick.

Second, an understanding of the fundamentals of a subject leads to a greater comprehension of the subject. These basic concepts serve as guideposts in helping the student through new material. Thus, instead of being faced with a sea of seemingly unrelated facts, the learner is able to perceive a pattern in them and a relationship between them. Many Christians avoid reading most of the Old Testament because they have never been shown the great themes, the big ideas, that run through the whole Bible. To persons without an understanding of these themes, the Old Testament remains a series of unrelated facts, instructions, and stories.

Third, a grasp of the basic concepts of a subject helps one to transfer learning, to apply the knowledge and skills learned in one particular setting to a new situation. Bruner suggests, "To understand something as a specific instance of a more general case—which is what understanding a more fundamental principle or structure means—is to have learned not only a specific thing but also a model for understanding other things like it that one may encounter" (1960, p. 25).

Our curriculum and our teaching must aim at communicating the big ideas of the faith (e.g., the nature of humans and the purpose of life). This does not mean that we cease to give attention to detail—we cannot, because basic concepts are formed only as facts are added together in a meaningful way. Details and specifics have to be attended to, but the emphasis must be on *appropriate* details, not *all* the details.

Time on Task

A review of research indicates that instruction time is a significant educational variable. Students tend to learn best the material that receives the greatest attention in the classroom. A subject on which a great deal of time is spent is better learned than subjects that are slighted. However, this rule does have its limit. There comes a point at which it falls victim to diminishing returns. Ten minutes added to a twenty-minute block of instruction is more likely to produce a measurable result than is ten minutes added to a two-hour lesson. Moreover, after a point, prolonging the instruction may actually have negative results (e.g., boredom).

Comprehensive studies such as those conducted by Jane Stallings and David Kaskowitz (1974) have consistently shown a strong relationship between time on task and academic achievement. Time spent on mathematics, reading, and other academic pursuits "yielded positive, significant, and consistent correlations" with academic achievement (Rosenshine 1976, p. 343); time given over to arts and crafts, playing with blocks, gazing into space, and self-discovery sessions did not. The message is clear: the more time given to academic activities, the greater the academic achievement.

In a recent comprehensive review of educational research on the relationship between the nature of instruction and student achievement, Jere Brophy and Thomas Good concluded that "the most consistently replicated findings link achievement to the quantity and pacing of instruction" (1986, p. 360). The amount of time given to the material to be mastered can properly be viewed as simply one dimension of the larger construct "quantity and pacing of instruction." The principle of allocating enough time to the material is emphasized here because it is so concrete and tangible—and so consistently violated in the practice of Christian education. Brophy and Good make several suggestions as to how the teacher might increase the time spent on the task at hand and thus enhance student learning (1986, pp. 360–61). The list is refreshingly concrete, and the general approach to teaching that it advocates can easily be explained to volunteer teachers. Furthermore, since these items are not restricted to a specific instructional method—they work whether the class centers around lectures, discussions, or projects—they do not threaten the teacher's time-honored practices. They may, however, challenge the teacher's style of classroom management and lesson planning.

Pace the instruction so that the students have ample opportunity to cover the material thoroughly.

Allocate the instructional time so as to emphasize the most significant topics in the curriculum.

Engage the students in learning tasks that are appropriately difficult. They need to cover the material with a sense of success and in graduated steps.

Take an active role. When allowed to go unsupervised, discussions and class projects do not foster the same quality of learning as when they are supervised by a teacher seeking to draw the learners into the activities.

In Christian education it is necessary to plan carefully so that the very limited amount of time available is put to the best possible use. In some cases the clearest way to address the problem of limited time is simply to carve out more time for educational activities. Many church-education programs are doomed to mediocrity from the beginning because of time restraints. Ensuring that enough time is afforded to the lesson is a matter of both educational planning (the Sunday school must be given enough time) and teaching skill (the instructor must be able to sustain the student's interest in a subject). Many teachers could improve their teaching by following two simple guidelines: work to protect instruction time from competing activities, and "major on the majors and minor on the minors" (i.e., know what is important and emphasize it). However, an educator must not let the restraints of time become an excuse for a get-down-to-business approach that robs Christian education of its proper caring and relational focus. On the other hand, although we may enjoy donuts, coffee, and opening exercises, it is to be remembered that there is a direct correlation between time spent on a lesson and the quality of learning.

Developmental Considerations

To live is to change. Our lives, from childhood through adulthood, are marked by transformation and growth. Developmental psychology studies this growth and seeks to describe the complex and puzzling age-related changes that occur throughout the life span. The time, processes, and results of developmental change are all scrutinized in the effort to understand this particular piece of the human puzzle. However, the descriptions of human development that come from the various schools of developmental psychology resemble the reports of the proverbial blind men and the elephant: their reports on the same creature are vastly different. In the current situation there simply is no universal developmental psychology but several theories that sometimes complement and sometimes conflict with one another. Recognizing this plurality of theories, we will restrict our discussion of human development to principles that enjoy broad support.

Two common misconceptions should be addressed at the start. First, developmental psychology does not maintain that children are quite limited in what they can learn. Many well-meaning educators have interpreted Piaget to say, "Children cannot do all that much, so leave them alone. You can teach them once they have developed." Such a position is promulgated in Ronald Goldman's *Readiness for Religion* (1965). Goldman argues that children see everything in concrete terms, including God as some sort of magical figure. If one teaches them abstract Christianity, their religious beliefs become hopelessly confused. Consequently, Goldman advocates waiting until adolescence before beginning Christian education. Jerome Bruner vigorously disagrees: "Any subject can be taught effectively in some intellectually honest form to any child at any stage of development. . . . No evidence exists to contradict it; considerable evidence is being amassed that supports it" (1960, p. 33). Developmental psychology has discovered age-related characteristics of thinking and learning, but not the age-related cognitive handicaps that Goldman and others have postulated.

The second misconception is that psychological development occurs according to a biological clock that all of us share. We see so much regularity in physical growth that it is natural to carry a similar expectation over to the psychological domain. However, psychological growth does not occur automatically. Just as biological growth cannot occur without food and relative health, psychological growth requires that individuals have a variety of experiences that enable them to develop attributes such as trust, love, and industry. The mere passage of time does not produce personal growth.

The study of human development has enriched Christian education by fostering a sensitive approach to the students. Christian-education programs that have been shaped by the study of human development tend to stress holism, age-appropriateness, enriching experiences that will promote growth, and correction of earlier misunderstandings.

Holism

Education is primarily concerned with shaping, informing, influencing, and developing the cognitive side of an individual; but every aspect of the learner has at least an indirect role to play in the accomplishment of this rather narrow task. Many of the findings of developmental psychology remind us that we are complex creatures whose minds and bodies and souls are bound together. Consequently, the teacher must consider the whole person. Paul wrote about certain individuals who were gifted to be "pastors and teachers" (Eph. 4:11), a very powerful combination of terms, for it captures the essence of Christian ministry to the whole person. It affirms the necessity of shepherding and caring for God's flock as well as teaching and instructing them.

Age-Appropriateness

Educational activities are described as age-appropriate if they can generally be accomplished in a meaningful way, without undue frustration, by children of a given age. (Since children differ from one another, it is impossible, of course, to identify highly specific tasks which all children of a certain age will relish and excel at.) The concept of age-appropriateness has been part of educational thought since ancient times. However, modern studies once again remind educators, and especially Christian educators, that children are not just little adults. Their world is not the same as that of adults, and their concerns are not to be summarily dismissed as being immature. Rather, their world and outlook must be the starting point for challenging these young disciples to a more complete understanding of their faith and its responsibilities.

Enriching Experiences

Human development does not take place automatically with the passage of time. Rather, human maturation results from growth-producing responses (obviously not all responses are growth-producing) to one's experiences. Developmental psychologists in the tradition of Jean Piaget have identified various ways of promoting human development. They have shown that schools can help foster human development, cognitive or spiritual, by providing rich experiences (not merely flashy experiences, which have little substance) and by helping the students reflect on what they have learned. The interaction between these new experiences and one's mental map promotes human development. Psychological and spiritual growth by and large result from the process of fine-tuning one's mental map so that it more adequately represents the way in which the world, including the spiritual realm, is actually arranged (Peck 1978).

Correction of Earlier Misunderstandings

Developmental psychology sees the learner as someone trying to make sense of the world. From time to time everyone misinterprets the available data and draws a faulty

conclusion, but if we are open to change, misunderstandings may well be corrected at a later time. I remember
that when I learned the Twenty-third Psalm as a first grader,
I was confused by the line "The LORD is my Shepherd; I
shall not want" (KJV). I reasoned that I should want the
Lord, but this psalm seemed to be saying that I should not
want him. The dissonance was not great enough to induce
me to ask an adult to help me out of this quandary, but
some years later when I relearned the psalm, I was reminded of my earlier misunderstanding. I corrected my
mistake on my own as I sought to understand the world
around me.

Folk wisdom has told us for years that good education
involves repetition. It was thought that repetition helps
students remember. Developmental psychology has shown
that when properly used, repetition does more than simply help a person remember. It gives one the opportunity
to examine from a more developed standpoint something
that was previously learned. Bruner refers to a "spiral curriculum": the same topic is re-presented to learners at
different ages so that they can think it through from their
more advanced perspective (1960, pp. 52–54). In a simple
way, I was exposed to a spiral curriculum in learning Psalm
23. Through such re-presentations students have the opportunity to work out earlier misunderstandings.

Attributes of Effective Teachers

What are the qualities of good teaching? Despite years
of research into this subject, the findings are surprisingly
ambiguous. It is difficult to define effective teaching on
the basis of social-science research. Yet the inconclusive
findings do tell us something important about the nature
of classroom teaching: it is very complex. The following
negative conclusions reflect some of the complexity of the
matter and eliminate some favorite myths about the marks
of good teaching:

No personality type can be singled out as making the best teachers.

No method of teaching can be singled out as the best.

Audio-visual devices and computer-aided instruction do not necessarily enhance learning.

Discussion-oriented teaching is not necessarily more meaningful than lecturing.

Class size does not necessarily affect the extent to which the material will be internalized.

Many similar findings could be listed. They suggest that there is no basis for much of the educational dogmatism that exists today. Teaching is complex and difficult (as well as quite rewarding), and it is open to a variety of personalities and classroom styles. The emphasis of this section is not on finding the nonexistent *best way* of teaching but on providing insights that may help teachers be more effective.

Although it is difficult to identify definitively the qualities of good teaching, we do know that both good and bad teaching are taking place in our churches today. Ineffective Christian teaching is nothing short of tragic. While it may not be a sin to bore people, it certainly is sinful to fail to equip Christians for serving Christ as believer-priests. Ineffective teaching can be corrected only by changing ineffective teachers into effective ones. That piece of advice may seem simplistic, yet many Christian-education programs have not heeded it. Most programs spend far more money on a four-color curriculum than they do on teacher training, in spite of the fact that the most important resource a Christian-education program has is its teachers. Classroom instruction will be only as effective as the teacher who provides it. Teacher training and proper evaluation of instruction are hard work, but they are mandatory if effective education is to take place.

Despite the general inconclusiveness, research does indicate that certain characteristics are essential if a teacher is to be effective. In a comprehensive review of fifty studies concerning instructional effectiveness, Barak Rosenshine and Norma Furst (1971) conclude that certain qualities in a teacher do enhance student learning. Their list, which is not intended to be comprehensive, is topped by clarity, enthusiasm, variability, and task-orientation. We will briefly explore a similar list of characteristics which a growing body of research regards as vital (Gephart, Strother, and Duckett 1981a).

Enthusiasm

Why enthusiasm is important in classroom teaching is hard to pinpoint, but there is general agreement that students think enthusiasm is important. That should not surprise us; almost everyone would prefer an animated, colorful, and dramatic presentation over one that is lifeless and dull. The real question is, To what extent are enthusiastic or charismatic teachers more effective than less dramatic teachers?

The traditional wisdom, which today enjoys some experimental support, maintains that enthusiastic teachers are more effective because they hold their students' attention, and students tend to project the positive feelings they have for charismatic teachers onto the material. An enthusiastic and witty literature professor is more likely to engender a positive attitude toward literature than is a dull and unimaginative teacher. Joseph Epstein's idea of what makes great teachers great centers on a balanced enthusiasm: "What all the great teachers appear to have in common is love of their subject, an obvious satisfaction in arousing this love in their students, and an ability to convince them that what they are being taught is deadly serious" (1981, p. xii).

An enthusiastic teacher has the power to captivate an audience:

Julius Miller was . . . a physics professor in Southern California who was a semi-regular on the old Steve Allen Tonight Show. Miller appeared from time to time on the show to demonstrate some physics principle. But he did more than demonstrate. He emoted an excitement for observing and understanding physics principles that hooked many of us who watched the show. One night he demonstrated the force of atmospheric pressure. A huge can was set on a rack with a fire under it. When steam boiled out of the can the fire was doused and a cap sealed the can. The sealed can was sprayed with a fire hose and before the viewers' eyes it crumpled. Miller jumped up and down in excitement and shouted, *"Look* at that!" It was patently clear to him that an important phenomenon was taking place, that we should see it and understand it. [Gephart, Strother, and Duckett 1981b, p. 1]

Miller's enthusiasm held people's attention on a subject they might otherwise have ignored. Also, he modeled a playful spirit of observation that marks science at its best.

Enthusiasm does have a negative side: it often masks ineffective teaching. Because students enjoy enthusiasm, it can help make teaching effective; but enthusiasm by itself is not synonymous with effective teaching. The confusion of enthusiastic and dramatic teaching with effective teaching has come to be known in educational circles as the Dr. Fox effect:

[A now famous study] found that an entertaining, charismatic lecturer who spoke deliberate nonsense received surprisingly high evaluations from an audience of educators and mental health professionals. Because the lecturer—actually a professional actor—was introduced as Dr. Myron L. Fox, the phenomenon became known as the "Dr. Fox" effect. . . . A lecturer's authority, wit, and personality can "seduce" students into the illusion of having learned, even when the educational content of the lecture was missing. [Abrami, Leventhal, and Perry 1982, p. 446]

Students are generally poor at discerning whether a teacher with high charisma has communicated any subject matter. It has been empirically demonstrated that they can easily confuse show with substance.

The classroom spellbinder may have little to offer besides a commanding voice, humorous gestures, and clever stories, despite the glowing reports the students give. Christian education is intended to equip and renew, not primarily to entertain; therefore, teacher evaluation must look at more than whether students enjoy the class. Enthusiasm should be fostered in teachers but never confused with truly effective teaching.

Enthusiasm is clearly more than a natural trait. In fact, teachers can be trained to be more enthusiastic (Bettencourt 1983). It is worth noting that our term *enthusiasm* comes from a Greek word meaning "inspired by a god," which suggests that an enthusiastic teacher is one who is inspired by another force. For most teachers that force is a love for the subject, for teaching itself, or for the students. In a very real sense, however, the enthusiasm of the Christian teacher should come from God the Holy Spirit. To be inspired by God (enthusiasm) is particularly important for Christian educators because a vital part of their responsibility to their students is to serve as models of the Christian life.

Clear Communication

Effective educators teach in such a way that their students understand the subject matter. Here again is a truth which needs some qualification: good teaching is far more than just clear explanation, and sometimes when teachers explain things too well, the students become passive and do not dig out answers on their own. Angus Taylor recalls that his brilliant Harvard math professor would tell his students, "The clearer the teacher makes it, the worse it is for you. You must work things out for yourself and make the ideas your own" (1984, p. 607). Yet without sufficient clarity of communication the teacher contributes very little. Good teaching is the facilitation of self-directed learning, and part—but not all—of that facilitation comes through clear explanations.

To be a clear communicator a teacher must possess strong oral skills and the ability to read the audience and respond appropriately. An effective teacher can read the audience by using questions well. Questions can check the students' level of understanding and can prompt them to think more deeply about a given subject. Ronald Hyman (1982, p. 1) suggests a number of reasons for using questions:

> To diagnose a student's degree or level of understanding of a concept or topic.

> To involve the student, help keep the student alert, or provide an opportunity for the student to shine in front of classmates.

> To determine the extent to which supplied data can be used to reason and solve problems.

> To review, restate, or summarize fundamental points from previous sessions.

> To provide a springboard for discussion, stimulate imagination, or obtain ideas to which class members can react.

> To maintain discipline or stop a student from disrupting the class.

Questions are also occasionally used by teachers to show off their knowledge or to put down students. This behavior has no place in education, especially in the church.

It has proven difficult to improve the question-asking facet of some teachers' instruction. Part of the reason may lie in the character or personality of the individual teacher. It is rather pointless to teach question-asking techniques to a teacher who does not really care what the students think. But for the teacher who does care, research studies do have a few suggestions (Henson 1979; Hyman 1979, 1982):

> Pause after asking a question. (Studies have found that many teachers wait less than two seconds before answering their own questions.)
>
> Ask only one question at a time.
>
> Do not expect students to be able to guess what is on your mind.
>
> Use a variety of questions, ranging from questions requiring recall of fact to questions requiring synthesis.
>
> Help a student modify an inaccurate answer until it becomes acceptable.

Research has not focused on the issue of how teachers can be clearer in their presentations. Part of the reason is that researchers have been looking for new and different ways of teaching. David Ausubel (1969), however, has spent considerable time and effort attempting to make the tried-and-true form of teaching even better. From his research and writing, four major attributes of clear teaching emerge.

First, clear teaching has what Ausubel calls an advance organizer, a special type of introduction that provides students with a framework on which to attach the material to be covered in a class. This introduction should present the principles or big ideas of the lecture rather than just an outline or summary. Second, clear and effective teaching shows how the parts relate to the whole. The listener understands how the various parts of the lesson fit together, for the teacher gives some verbal cues at transition points and periodically summarizes what has been covered. Third, clear instruction limits the amount of material covered. Novice teachers typically try to cover far too much content. Quality learning is more important than quantity. Fourth, clear teaching focuses on what is meaningful. Students find presentations of meaningful material to be far clearer and more understandable than presentations of material they judge to be irrelevant.

Without clarity, effective teaching is impossible; with it, the foundation is laid for productive instruction. Perhaps the best way to ensure clear teaching is to keep in view a picture of the major contrasts between clear and unclear teaching (Gephart, Strother, and Duckett 1981a, 1981b):

Marks of Clear Teaching	Marks of Unclear Teaching
Use of demonstrations and illustrations	Vagueness in expression
Fluency in presentation	Mazes and blind alleys in the presentation
Thorough grasp of material	Lack of assurance regarding the material
Appropriate redundancy	An attempt to cover too much too fast
Careful monitoring of student learning	Unawareness or misreading of student cues
Appropriate organization	Lack of organization

Understanding of the Subject Matter

Effective teachers have a firm grasp on the subject matter they are teaching. In a comprehensive review of the lecture method, John McLeish notes that "students regarded effective teaching as being the result of *knowledge* of the subject, *organization* and method in presenting it, and *commitment* to the area of specialization" (1976,

p. 299). Without a firm grasp of the subject matter, teachers are unable to think on their feet and adapt to their class, but most important, they will not be able to focus on the big ideas. A teacher to whom the subject matter is a fog will probably focus on highly specific facts or else make broad generalizations that are not meaningful to the students.

High Expectations

Effective teachers expect good things to happen, and then they make them happen. To a large extent, ineffective teaching is a self-fulfilling prophecy. If teachers do not expect much learning to take place, it generally will not. While high expectations do not guarantee effectiveness, they do play a major role in student achievement.

In *Pygmalion in the Classroom* Robert Rosenthal and Lenore Jacobson (1968) describe the now famous experiment in which they demonstrated a link between teacher expectations and student performance. Students in eighteen classes were administered a standard test of verbal intelligence. Their teachers were led to believe that this test would help identify those students who were about to bloom academically. The experimenters labeled 20 percent of the students as potential bloomers. These students, however, were selected at random and with no regard to the test scores—a fact of which the teachers were unaware. A readministration of the same test some eight months later showed marked differences in intellectual growth between the supposed bloomers and the rest of the students. Similar experimental evidence strongly supports the notion that achievement is highly related to the expectations of the teacher. Teachers who expect great things often act to fulfil their prophecy.

Formality and Flexibility

Although no teaching method can be singled out as the best, there is mounting empirical evidence (and plenty of

folk wisdom) to suggest that formal methods of instruction are more effective than informal ones. This principle
holds true whether the desired outcome be knowledge,
creativity, or social stability. Formal methods involve more
teacher control of the class and use more-traditional assignments. These findings seem to be true especially of
the elementary grades, where students in an informal
classroom often squander the freedom they are given. Many
students find informal classrooms to be anxiety-producing
because there is a lack of stability, the rules of conduct
are often not clearly defined, and some children use their
freedom to abuse others.

In one of the more ambitious studies to date, Neville
Bennett found that teachers who use formal methods, that
is, whose instruction is marked by "teacher directed manner with the accent on the acquisition of basic skills and
knowledge to specified levels of achievement" (1976, p. 64),
are far more effective than teachers whose approach is
more informal. The intriguing aspect of this study is that
students' performance was measured by tests which each
teaching orientation (i.e., formal, informal, and mixed)
saw as valid. The formal classroom did the best in terms
of reading and math skills, creativity, expository writing,
and other basic areas (p. 152). The results of this study are
clear, and more-recent studies point in the same direction:
teachers who are appropriately task-oriented are more effective. (It is possible, of course, to *appear* casual and yet
have goals clearly in mind. Captain Kangaroo and Mister
Rogers, for example, obviously set agendas for their tele-
vision programs yet do not discuss them on the show.
Such planned and goal-directed informality makes them
appear more natural.)

Why do teachers who use formal methods do so well?
The research really stops short of answering that question,
but their success may be due to their possessing a greater
sense of the direction in which they want to guide the
student. They plan more, and they tend to spend more

time mastering the material they teach. The results of this study and similar ones, however, are probably highly age-related. While the success of formal instruction of children may be clear, there is mounting evidence that adults thrive in a more open learning environment (Knowles 1973). But even in an informal setting, clarity and planning are still vital if the teacher's presentations are to be effective.

Much wisdom is required in trying to find a proper balance between formal and informal approaches. Teachers who rely on formal methods can certainly learn much from those who use more-informal methods and who understand what it means to be flexible. Christian educators are not teaching theology but Christian living, and they must be willing to seize the teachable moments at hand. Too many formally oriented teachers are so intent on getting through the lesson that they forget to focus on the meaningfulness of the material. Informally oriented teachers are often so captured by the moment that their students gain little formal understanding of the faith. Changing mental maps, equipping believer-priests for service, and helping pilgrims on their way are hard tasks, and those teachers who are caught up solely in the urgent and the relevant will often fail at these tasks. Only by maintaining a balance between the formal and informal will Christian educators fulfil their awesome responsibilities.

= 8 =

Toward an Evangelical Theory of Biblical Instruction

A theory of education must be clear enough for a teacher to carry into the classroom without having to consult a large number of books, and it must accurately reflect the real world so that the teacher is not torn between theory and reality. A good theory is like a good map: it gives a person guidance, helps one know what to expect next, and lets one see the big picture instead of drowning in a sea of facts.

This chapter is an integration of theology, educational theory, and social science into an evangelical theory of biblical instruction. Christian education involves more than teaching the Bible, but teaching it is a mandatory part of any Christian-education program worthy of the name. The Christian educator who considers this awesome responsibility must ask, How can I make sure my teaching of the Bible helps students to detect God's purpose and meaning for their lives and promotes Christian maturity? The teacher must never forget that the Bible is a tool not only to increase our knowledge of Scripture, but to promote spiritual maturity as well. When the Bible is so used in the Christian-education process, there will be various evidences in the lives of the students: biblical literacy, a delight in Scripture, submission to the Bible, an appropriate method of interpreting it, a Christian worldview, and use of God's Word as a spiritual tool.

Biblical Literacy

The first, though not the primary, objective of biblical instruction must be biblical literacy. If students are to live as responsible Christians, it is necessary for them to act according to biblical principles, which in turn requires a knowledge of the content of the Bible. If one does not know what the Bible says, it is impossible to obey it. Such a statement is a truism, yet many Christians are so ignorant of the principles of the Bible that they cannot speak in any meaningful way of being in submission to the Scriptures. Like the Hebrews before us, we should be known as "people of the Book." A necessary (but not sufficient) prerequisite is biblical literacy.

Consider the findings from a 1980 Gallup poll of 1,030 teenagers. The report opens with these sobering words: "Few trends in religion so threaten to undermine organized religion in the 1980s as does the sorry state of biblical knowledge in our nation" (Princeton Religion Research Center 1981, p. 1). The results of this study are quite astounding, for they reveal that many church-attending teens do not have a grasp of the essentials of the faith. For example, the respondents were asked three simple questions about the New Testament: to name the four Gospels, give the number of Christ's disciples, and identify the event commemorated at Easter. Table 5 illustrates the dearth of religious knowledge in contemporary America. Fully 20 percent of the teenagers in this study who attended church regularly could not name the event that Easter commemorates. The research analyst said it well: "The fact that 29% of all teenagers—and 20% of those

TABLE 5 **American Teenagers' Knowledge of the New Testament**

	Questions			
	Four Gospels	*Number of Disciples*	*Easter Event*	*All Three*
Regular church attenders	50%	81%	80%	43%
Nonattenders	19%	50%	61%	16%
All	35%	66%	71%	30%

From Princeton Religion Research Center, *PRRC Emerging Trends* 3.5 (1981).

who attend religious services regularly—didn't know what Easter commemorates will be shocking to Christian leaders" (p. 1).

The most disquieting aspect of this study is that many young people who say they believe in the authority of the Bible do not know what it says. For example, a large majority (79 percent) of the teens interviewed said they believed that the Ten Commandments provide valuable guidance for today. However, they could name, on the average, only four of the commandments. Although the Ten Commandments were regarded as a valid moral guideline, only 3 percent of the teens could name all ten (Princeton Religion Research Center 1981, p. 4). Religious knowledge is at a low point in our country, and not just among teenagers. As we survey the ills and injustices of our secular society, let us not be too quick to conclude that the Bible is powerless to undo the evils of the world. The reason the Bible has not been an overpowering force in today's world is that only a precious few have a substantial knowledge of God's Word.

For a variety of reasons, most Christian educators today do not stress the concept of biblical literacy. Their chief aim is the development of "healthy relationships." Consequently, self-understanding, interpersonal skills, and caring for others are the focus of Christian education far more often than is biblical literacy. (We might question whether self-understanding is possible when one is ignorant of the biblical understanding of God and human nature.) To many Christian educators biblical literacy smacks of an outmoded provincialism which naively assumed that cognitive knowledge can have a positive impact upon one's life. Religious educators today tend to view factual knowledge as being sterile and as having little capacity to change a person's life. It would seem that texts like "For as he thinks within himself, so he is" (Prov. 23:7, NASB) have been forgotten. Modern liberal religion and most Christian educators (whether liberal or conservative) see the essence of religion as being the will and emotions. These dimensions of our personhood are thought to be affected far more by our glands than by our minds. Now we certainly cannot claim that Christianity is primarily a religion of the mind. Yet it is a religion that demands subordination of the will and emotions to the truths of Scripture, which are perceived by the mind, and to the leading of the Holy Spirit. Biblical literacy, then, is an absolutely essential first step toward ordering our lives according to God's will.

A Delight in Scripture

Christian education must engender a delight in reading and studying the Bible. Bible reading out of compliance or for the sake of reward falls off quickly when the external incentive (e.g., teacher praise or gold stars) is no longer a factor. We must adopt educational strategies which encourage persons to find spiritual refreshment and nourishment in the Scriptures. Such intrinsic motivation will attract Christians throughout their lives to this life-changing book. With David, Christians should find God's Word to be "more precious than gold" and "sweeter than honey" (Ps. 19:10).

One way in which a teacher can promote a delight in reading and studying the Bible is to be an example. If the class can see that their teacher is excited about the Bible and finds it to be a source of spiritual refreshment and nourishment, they are more likely to turn to the Bible with an expectancy of finding spiritual refreshment. Modeling a positive attitude toward the Bible can be infectious.

Another way to promote a delight in Scripture is to utilize external motivations. I often meet college students who for the first time in their lives are excited about great literature, largely because they have been placed in a situation where they have to read it. People can never develop a love for Scripture without having read it. Crass forms of external motivation such as prizes and trinkets, which usually turn the class into speed-readers or liars, should be avoided. The focus should be on the joy of reading and studying the Bible on one's own. It is sometimes appropriate to hold older students accountable for doing some preparatory reading (e.g., the teacher could limit class participation to those who have read the lesson). Accountability is not the whole answer, but it gives some people a push who would never open the Bible on a regular basis without it.

Submission to the Bible

Christian education must foster a humble submission to the Bible's authority. The Bible can play its God-intended role in the believer's life only when it is viewed as "the rule of faith and practice." The question of how such a disposition can be cultivated is not easily answered. The two usual answers—through verbal assent (i.e., by declaring, "The Bible is authoritative in my life") and behavior modification—are only half answers at best. Both fall short of instilling a genuine submission to the Bible, and neither one equips the Christian to use the Bible as the final authority in the difficult situations of life.

True submission to the Word of God requires (1) a heart-felt recognition of its authority and (2) the skill and habit of reflecting on life's experiences in light of the Bible. Christians need to be encouraged to make a Scripture-based evaluation of their actions and beliefs. This evaluation should lead to the alteration of beliefs and behaviors found to be out of harmony with the Bible. Only through a thoughtful reflection on the compatibility (or lack of compatibility) between one's practices and the norms of Scripture does the Bible become authoritative in one's life. Unfortunately, our television-dependent nation does not encourage reflection on our life in light of our declared values and priorities. But even though reflection may not come easily, it is essential to Christian living.

Such interaction between the Bible and life was advocated by the biblical authors themselves. A clear example is found in the Book of James. After arguing that Christians must "not merely listen to the word" but "do what it says" (James 1:22), James describes a chief difference between those who merely hear the Bible and those who actually do what it says. Those who only hear the Bible are like a man who just glances at his reflection in a mirror and goes on his way. He does nothing to improve his appearance. The effectual doer, on the other hand, "looks intently into the perfect law" (v. 25). He looks long and hard at the image in the mirror and thus comes to see what the law requires and how he is actually living. He recognizes the disparity between his life and God's requirement. As we rearrange our attire after studying ourselves in a mirror, so also should we change our lives after studying our actions and priorities in the mirror of God's Word.

A good teacher not only informs the students about the contents of the Bible, but also seeks to help them view their present attitudes, actions, and circumstances in the light of its teachings. The prophet Haggai challenged the people of Israel to reflect on their current plight: "Give careful thought to your ways. You have planted much, but have harvested little. You eat, but never have enough" (Hag. 1:5–6). Haggai was called by God to preach to the nation of Israel after it had returned from exile in Babylon. The people had become discouraged in the process of rebuilding the temple and had turned instead to their own businesses, home building, and daily routines. As a result, the Lord not only withheld his blessing, but brought a famine to the land for the purpose of waking up his people. Haggai knew that the people did not need just to hear the Word of the Lord; they needed to see the connection between their neglect of the temple and the hard times they were experiencing.[1]

Like the prophets of old, teachers must assist their students to see the differences between the theology of their talk and the theology of their walk. What leads to spiritual transformation is not a passive absorbing of Bible facts, but thoughtful reflection on what the Bible demands and promises and how we actually live. Fostering personal reflection on Scripture is part of the "ministry of meaning" to which Christian education is called.

An Appropriate Method of Interpretation

Protestants have been quicker to assert the right and responsibility of direct personal Bible study than actually to equip their laity for this task. Pastors typically exhort their parishioners to read and study the Bible and are distressed when they find that their advice has not been followed. But they seldom provide a method for reading and studying. For many Christians the Bible remains a strange and foreign book. Despite their affirmations that it is their rule of faith and practice, many read it with the disconcerting feeling that its shepherds, kings, and countless battles are largely irrelevant to modern life.

1. Thomas Groome (1981) has developed an educational strategy ("shared praxis") which focuses on the interaction between the Christian story and our lives.

Pastors know all too well how complex the task of interpreting the Bible has become as a result of modern biblical scholarship. The biblical languages, a knowledge of geography and ancient customs, archaeological finds, and textual studies all can enlighten the biblical text. While enlightening, however, they vastly complicate the process of interpretation. The bewildering task of biblical interpretation as that discipline exists today has caused some pastors to conclude that it should be left to the professionals. So they work hard on their sermons and teaching assignments in order to open the dark and mysterious Scriptures to the ordinary Christian. However, the consumption of good teaching or preaching is not a substitute for personal study. Luther was distressed when he saw how the church's emphasis on the Fathers had kept people from the Bible:

> The writings of all the holy fathers should be read only for a time, in order that through them we may be led to the Holy Scriptures. As it is, however, we read them only to be absorbed in them and never come to the Scriptures. We are like men who study the sign-posts and never travel the road. The dear fathers wished, by their writings, to lead us to the Scriptures, but we so use them as to be led away from the Scriptures, though the Scriptures alone are our vineyard in which we ought all to work and toil. [Luther 1982, p. 151]

It is equally tragic when pastors view the complexities of modern biblical scholarship as a reason for discouraging laypersons from investigating the Scriptures. A travelogue is not travel, a restaurant review is not a gourmet meal, and a sermon is not personal Bible study. Laypersons need to be trained and equipped to engage the biblical text themselves.

In training students to engage the Bible, the Christian educator must be mindful that in order for the Bible to have proper authority in their lives, they must be equipped with a proper method of interpretation. Humans are remarkably expert at making excuses and are capable of rationalizing any wrongful desire or behavior. Consequently, the system of interpretation that we use and model before lay Christians must be of such a nature as to ensure against a watering down or distortion of Scripture as a result of our human propensity to avoid the sharp sting of God's judgments or as a result of our own cultural rootedness, which can lead to self-serving interpretations. We are so much a part of our culture that it is difficult not to read our own cultural practices back into the Bible.

Far too many of the interpretive schemes used in modern Christian education are so utterly subjective that they dull the sharp edge of the Spirit's sword and rob the Bible of its force. The idiosyncratic spiritualizing found in many Christian-education curriculum materials provides very poor examples of Bible-study methods. We cannot endorse the notion that there is a professional approach to the Scriptures and a radically different lay approach. The trained clergy and scholars have knowledge, skills, and tools at their disposal that are not available to the typical layperson, but that does not mean that ordinary Christians must approach the Bible in some second-class manner. They can apply the same basic strategies and techniques that pastors and scholars use—but they must be trained to do so. Teaching Christians how to read and study the Bible is as important as teaching them Bible knowledge. Much Christian education, however, focuses on feeding Christians rather than on equipping them to feed themselves.

A Christian World-View

The quality of our existence depends on our perspective and our response to what life brings us. True contentment, happiness, and joy are not so much the product of our circumstances as they are the product of our responses to our circumstances. From our culture we inherit an essentially secular and humanistic world-view which at many points clashes with the gospel. As Christians we must reject the powerful secular view of ethics and the purpose of life (epitomized in statements like, "If it feels good, do it," and "You only go around once, so grab all the gusto you can") and embrace truly biblical concepts.

Christians need to learn to describe and evaluate life's experiences from a biblical perspective. Viewing a particular experience from a Christian standpoint can be truly liberating. The Christian is able to see pain as a time of potential growth, death as a new beginning, and the injustice in this world as ultimately being set aright. Few non-Christians are able to rise above their circumstances in the way that Christians can. A true Christian perspective on life helps free one from circumstances.

It is not easy to instill this perspective. In fact, developing a mature Christian world-view takes a lifetime. It requires teachers who not only are sensitive to the student's situation but who also can think theologically. One of the clearest presentations of the importance of teaching life-encompassing concepts in Christian education is Donald Joy's *Meaningful Learning in the Church.* In this book he argues that learning the "Big Ideas" of the Christian faith (e.g., the nature of God, humankind, sin, salvation, and the world) should be a major concern of Christian education, both because they will shape our view of the world, and because focusing on the big ideas makes good sense educationally. Educational research has taught us that unattached facts have a very short half-life. As Joy observes, "A 'fact' in isolation is almost certainly doomed to extinction, but if it can be filed with related material, it stands a fair chance for survival as a distinct fact" (1969, p. 55). When a teacher can help a student attach a piece of information to a broader concept, its likelihood of being remembered increases dramatically. Further, it will then play its own small part in shaping the student's world-view.

Use of Scripture as a Spiritual Tool

Christian educators must teach the Bible in such a way that their students learn how to use it as a spiritual tool, for the Bible is to be the Christian's chief spiritual instrument. While Christians must be literate in the Bible, they also must be able to use it effectively for the purposes for which it is intended. Alfred North Whitehead said, "Education is the acquisition of the art of the utilisation of knowledge" (1929, p. 4). The Bible is a multipurpose spiritual tool: it can properly be used to comfort, challenge, console, or spiritually refresh. In his numerous books Randolph Crump Miller reiterates the point that knowledge of the Bible and of theology is not to be seen as an end in itself: "The task of Christian education is not to teach theology, but to use theology as the basic tool for bringing learners into the right relationship with God in the fellowship of the church" (1950, p. 6). The apostle Paul also saw the Bible as a spiritual tool: "All Scripture is God-breathed and is useful for teaching, rebuking, correcting and training in righteousness, so that the man of God may be thoroughly equipped for every good work" (2 Tim. 3:16–17).

A maturing Christian is one who is learning to use the Bible to perform its intended spiritual work. The educational implications of this are quite clear. Just as a would-be physician cannot learn to use the tools of medicine merely by observing a doctor at work, neither can a Christian learn to use the Bible through observation alone. Modeling, instruction, practice, and supervision are all necessary to produce journeymen Bible-users. The training must begin by aiming at biblical literacy, but we cannot be content until we have equipped students to use their chief spiritual tool to the fullest degree. Believer-priests are called to a wide-ranging biblical ministry. Accordingly, Christian education in many ways must be more akin to an apprenticeship program than to an academic classroom. For Christians must not just learn about the Bible, but must learn to use the Bible, both in ordering their own lives and in ministering to others.

Bibliography

Abrami, P., L. Leventhal, and R. Perry. 1982. Educational seduction. *Review of Educational Research* 52: 446–64.

Achtemeier, E. 1962. Righteousness in the Old Testament. In *The interpreter's dictionary of the Bible,* edited by G. Buttrick, vol. 4. Nashville: Abingdon.

Adler, M. 1982. *The paideia proposal: An educational manifesto.* New York: Macmillan.

American Sunday School Union. 1833. *The ninth annual report of the American Sunday School Union.* Philadelphia.

Ausubel, D. 1969. *Readings in school learning.* New York: Holt, Rinehart & Winston.

Barringer, F., and B. Vobejda. 1985. Franchising Christian schools: Teacherless program pulled in about $22 million in '84. *Washington Post National Weekly Edition,* 18 March 1985.

Bennett, N. 1976. *Teaching styles and pupil progress.* Cambridge, Mass.: Harvard University Press.

Bettencourt, E., M. Gillett, M. Gall, and R. Hull. 1983. Effects of teacher enthusiasm training on student-on-task behavior and achievement. *American Educational Research Journal* 20: 435–50.

Bietenhard, H. 1976. Lord. In *The new international dictionary of New Testament theology,* edited by C. Brown, vol. 2. Grand Rapids: Zondervan.

Blackman, E. 1950. Knowledge. In *A theological word book of the Bible,* edited by A. Richardson. New York: Macmillan.

Bloesch, D. 1979. *Essentials of evangelical theology.* Vol. 1, *God, authority, salvation.* New York: Harper & Row.

Boden, M. 1979. *Jean Piaget.* New York: Viking.

Bransford, J. 1979. *Human cognition: Learning, understanding, and remembering.* Belmont, Calif.: Wadsworth.

Brophy, J., and T. Good. 1986. Teacher behavior and student achievement. In *Handbook of research on teaching,* 3d ed., edited by M. Wittrock. New York: Macmillan.

Brownell, W., and H. Moser. 1949. *Meaningful versus mechanical learning. A study in grade III subtraction.* Duke University Research Studies in Education 8. Durham, N.C.: Duke University Press.

Bruner, J. 1960. *The process of education.* Cambridge, Mass.: Harvard University Press.

————. 1966. *Toward a theory of instruction.* Cambridge, Mass.: Harvard University Press.

Bushnell, H. 1979. *Christian nurture.* Grand Rapids: Baker. Originally published 1861.

Calvin, J. 1960. *Institutes of the Christian religion.* Translated by F. Battles and edited by J. McNeill. Philadelphia: Westminster. Originally published 1559.

Coe, G. 1917. *A social theory of religious education.* New York: Scribner.

Cox, E. 1966. *Changing aims in religious education.* London: Routledge and Kegan Paul.

Crabb, L. 1988. *Inside out.* Colorado Springs: NavPress.

Cronbach, L. 1963. *Educational psychology.* 2d ed. New York: Harcourt, Brace & World.

Dewey, J. 1938. *Experience and education.* New York: Macmillan.

Edwards, A. 1941. Rationalization in recognition as a result of a political frame of reference. *Journal of Abnormal and Behavioral Psychology* 4: 224–35.

Epstein, J., ed. 1981. *Masters: Portraits of great teachers.* New York: Basic Books.

Ericksen, S. 1984. *The essence of good teaching.* San Francisco: Jossey-Bass.

Forman, G., and D. Kuschner. 1977. *The child's construction of knowledge: Piaget for teaching children.* Monterey, Calif.: Brooks/Cole.

Frankena, W. 1965. *Philosophy of education.* New York: Macmillan.

Frankl, V. 1963. *Man's search for meaning.* New York: Pocket Books.

Fry, J. 1961. *A hard look at adult Christian education.* Philadelphia: Westminster.

Gephart, W., D. Strother, and W. Duckett. 1981a. Practical applications of research. March 1981 newsletter of the Phi Delta Kappa Center on Evaluation, Development, and Research.

————. 1981b. Practical applications of research. June 1981 newsletter of the Phi Delta Kappa Center on Evaluation, Development, and Research.

Goldman, R. 1965. *Readiness for religion: A basis for developmental religious education.* New York: Seabury.

Griffin, E. 1982. *Getting together.* Downers Grove, Ill.: Inter-Varsity.

Griggs, D. 1977. *Twenty new ways of teaching the Bible.* Nashville: Abingdon.

Groome, T. 1981. *Christian religious education.* New York: Harper & Row.

Hall, G. S. 1901. The ideal school based on child study. *Forum* 32: 24–39.

Harrison, C. 1980. *Readability in the classroom.* Cambridge: Cambridge University Press.

Henderlite, R. 1964. *The Holy Spirit in Christian education.* Philadelphia: Westminster.

Henson, K. 1979. Questioning as a mode of instruction. *Clearinghouse* 53: 14–16.

Holmes, A. 1977. *All truth is God's truth.* Grand Rapids: Eerdmans.

Howard, W. 1973. Bible studies for small groups. *Faith-at-Work,* February 1973.

Hyde, D. 1966. *Dedication and leadership.* Notre Dame, Ind.: University of Notre Dame Press.

Hyman, R. 1979. *Strategic questioning.* Englewood Cliffs, N.J.: Prentice-Hall.

―――――. 1982. Questioning in the college classroom. Idea paper, August 1982.

Joy, D. 1969. *Meaningful learning in the church.* Winona Lake, Ind.: Light & Life.

Kierkegaard, S. 1941. *For self-examination and Judge for yourselves.* Translated by W. Lowrie. Princeton, N.J.: Princeton University Press. Originally published 1851.

Knowles, M. 1973. *The adult learner: A neglected species.* Houston: Gulf.

Kohlberg, L. 1968. The child as a moral philosopher. *Psychology Today* 2 (Sept. 1968): 25–30.

―――――, and R. Mayer. 1972. Development as the aim of education. *Harvard Educational Review* 42: 449–96.

Krutch, J. W. 1954. *The measure of man.* New York: Bobbs-Merrill.

Kuhn, T. 1970. *The structure of scientific revolutions.* 2d ed. Chicago: University of Chicago Press.

Kurtines, W., and E. Greif. 1974. The development of moral thought: Review and evaluation of Kohlberg's approach. *Psychological Bulletin* 81: 453–70.

LeBar, L. 1981. *Education that is Christian.* Old Tappan, N.J.: Revell.

Lee, J. 1973. *The flow of religious instruction: A social-science approach.* Dayton: Pflaum.

Levine, J., and G. Murphy. 1943. The learning and forgetting of controversial material. *Journal of Abnormal and Social Psychology* 38: 507–17.

Lewis, C. S. 1946. *The great divorce.* New York: Macmillan.

———. 1953. *The silver chair.* New York: Macmillan.

Lightfoot, J. 1869. *St. Paul's Epistle to the Philippians.* London: Macmillan.

Lindblom, C., and D. Cohen. 1979. *Usable knowledge: Social science and problem solving.* New Haven, Conn.: Yale University Press.

Luther, M. 1982. An open letter to the Christian nobility. In *Works of Martin Luther,* vol. 2. Grand Rapids: Baker. Originally published 1520.

Lynn, R., and E. Wright. 1980. *The big little school.* Rev. ed. Nashville: Abingdon.

McLeish, J. 1976. The lecture method. In *The psychology of teaching methods: Seventy-fifth yearbook of the National Society for the Study of Education,* edited by N. Gage, part 1. Chicago: University of Chicago Press.

Manson, T. 1958. *Ministry and priesthood: Christ's and ours.* London: Epworth.

Marshall, H. 1981. Open classrooms: Has the term outlived its usefulness? *Review of Educational Research* 51: 181–92.

Miller, R. 1950. *The clue to Christian education.* New York: Scribner.

———. 1956. *Education for Christian living.* Englewood Cliffs, N.J.: Prentice-Hall.

Niles, D. 1958. *Studies in Genesis.* Philadelphia: Westminster.

Packer, J. I. 1973. *Knowing God.* Downers Grove, Ill.: Inter-Varsity.

———. 1979. *God has spoken.* Downers Grove, Ill.: Inter-Varsity.

Peck, M. S. 1978. *The road less traveled: A new psychology of love, traditional values, and spiritual growth.* New York: Simon & Schuster.

Peters, T., and R. Waterman, Jr. 1982. *In search of excellence: Lessons from America's best-run companies.* New York: Warner.

Piaget, J., and B. Inhelder. 1973. *Memory and intelligence.* New York: Basic Books.

Plueddemann, J., and C. Plueddemann. 1990. *Pilgrims in progress: Growing through groups.* Wheaton, Ill.: Harold Shaw.

Princeton Religion Research Center. 1981. *PRRC Emerging Trends* 3.5. Princeton, N.J.

Rosenshine, B. 1976. Classroom instruction. In *The psychology of teaching methods: Seventy-fifth yearbook of the National Society for the Study of Education,* edited by N. Gage, part 1. Chicago: University of Chicago Press.

_____. 1979. Content, time, and direct instruction. In *Research on teaching: Concepts, findings, and implications,* edited by P. Peterson and H. Walberg. Berkeley: McCutchan.

_____, and N. Furst. 1971. Research in teacher performance criteria. In *Research in teacher education: A symposium,* edited by B. Smith. Englewood Cliffs, N.J.: Prentice-Hall.

Rosenthal, R., and L. Jacobson. 1968. *Pygmalion in the classroom: Teacher expectation and pupils' intellectual development.* New York: Holt, Rinehart & Winston.

Rousseau, J. J. 1962. *Emile.* Translated and edited by W. Boyd. New York: Columbia University Press. Originally published 1762.

Ryken, L. 1984. *How to read the Bible as literature.* Grand Rapids: Zondervan.

Schmidt, K. 1963. *Kaleō.* In *Theological dictionary of the New Testament,* edited by G. Kittel, translated by G. Bromiley, vol. 3. Grand Rapids: Eerdmans. Originally published 1933.

Schmidt, S. 1983. *A history of the Religious Education Association.* Birmingham, Ala.: Religious Education Press.

Schuller, R. 1982. *Self-esteem.* Waco, Tex.: Word.

Skinner, B. F. 1971. *Beyond freedom and dignity.* New York: Bantam.

Soltis, J. 1978. *An introduction to the analysis of educational concepts.* 2d ed. Reading, Mass.: Addison-Wesley.

Spener, J. 1964. *Pia desideria.* Translated and edited by T. Tappert. Philadelphia: Fortress. Originally published 1675.

Sproul, R. C. 1977. *Knowing Scripture.* Downers Grove, Ill.: InterVarsity.

Stallings, J., and D. Kaskowitz. 1974. *Follow-through classroom observation evaluation—1972–1973.* Menlo Park, Calif.: Stanford Research Institute.

Steinkamp, M., and M. Maehr. 1983. Affect, ability, and science achievement: A quantitative synthesis of correlational research. *Review of Education Research* 53: 369–96.

Stott, J. 1961. *Preacher's portrait.* Grand Rapids: Eerdmans.

Taylor, A. 1984. A life in mathematics remembered. *American Math Monthly* 91: 605–17.

Torrance, T. F. 1955. *Royal priesthood.* Scottish Journal of Theology Occasional Papers 3. Edinburgh: Oliver and Boyd.

Ward, T., and S. Rowen. 1972. The significance of the extension seminary. *Evangelical Missions Quarterly* 9.1: 17–27.

Ward, W., and P. Barcher. 1975. Reading achievement and creativity as related to open classroom experience. *Journal of Educational Psychology* 67: 683–91.

Whitehead, A. 1929. *The aims of education.* New York: Free Press.

Wilhoit, J. 1983a. An examination of the educational principles and assumptions of an early nineteenth century Sunday school curriculum: *The Union Questions.* Ph.D. dissertation, Northwestern University.

————. 1983b. Memory: An area of difference between Piaget and Goldman. *Journal of Christian Education* 2: 11–14.

————. 1984. The impact of the social sciences on religious education. *Religious Education* 79: 367–75.

Willard, D. 1988. *The spirit of the disciplines.* New York: Harper & Row.

Wink, W. 1973. *The Bible in human transformation.* Philadelphia: Fortress.

Wolterstorff, N. 1980. *Educating for responsible action.* Grand Rapids: Eerdmans.

————. 1984. *Reason within the bounds of religion.* 2d ed. Grand Rapids: Eerdmans.

Zuck, R. 1972. *Spiritual power in your teaching.* Chicago: Moody.

Zwingli, U. 1953. Of the clarity and certainty of the Word of God. In *Zwingli and Bullinger,* edited and translated by G. Bromiley. Philadelphia: Westminster. Originally published 1522.

Index

177